Words of Praise...

Greg Birkett is a phenomenal writer. Gifted with a dynamic way of captivating his audience, while giving them a unique glimpse into the brilliant and vibrant canvas of his mind.

With every poem, monologue and litany; you can hear, see and feel his undeniable conviction.

Each piece, carrying its own profound weight as you're drawn into reading the next 'Conversation'. Greg has truly been given a gift *"His tongue is the pen of a ready writer"* Psalms 45.

~ **Judith James**, Ordained Pastor,
Founder and President - The Beautiful Foundation

Blessed with the gift of communication, Greg Birkett delivers pieces that flow effortlessly from the pen of a consummate chronicler and orator. In this work, he blends the artistic with the mundane to challenge prevailing opinions and increase awareness in multiple areas that apply for attention persistently. Readers will not be disappointed as they immerse themselves repeatedly in this masterful creation.

~ **Maria McClean**, RN, MDiv., DMin, BCCC, BCPC,
Director, Health and Prayer Ministries
Ontario Conference

You're holding in your hand a life-changing book. I know that from my own experience. I can vividly re-call the day I read this book. What I thought was just another typical day; I now see was actually the first step on a journey that would take me full circle to where I fell in love with the artistry of writing and God's word. The reference to music and miraculously merging it to today's logical linguistic approach is brilliant. The biblically blending bravery of hermeneutical credence is honored. This book is both educational and eternally appealing. Prepare your heart to be thrilled into a memory of who our God is, was and forever will be.

~ **Marvin G. Clarke Sr.**, Ordained Minister,
Philanthropist, Ph. Candidate in Counseling &
CEO of CHANGE4UTODAY & Speaker

When He Speaks, I Write

GREGORY BIRKETT

TEACH Services, Inc.
P U B L I S H I N G
www.TEACHServices.com • (800) 367-1844

World rights reserved. This book or any portion thereof may not be copied or reproduced in any form or manner whatever, except as provided by law, without the written permission of the publisher, except by a reviewer who may quote brief passages in a review.

The author assumes full responsibility for the accuracy of all facts and quotations as cited in this book. The opinions expressed in this book are the author's personal views and interpretations, and do not necessarily reflect those of the publisher.

This book is provided with the understanding that the publisher is not engaged in giving spiritual, legal, medical, or other professional advice. If authoritative advice is needed, the reader should seek the counsel of a competent professional.

Copyright © 2023 Gregory Birkett
Copyright © 2023 TEACH Services, Inc.
ISBN-13: 978-1-4796-1363-2 (Paperback)
ISBN-13: 978-1-4796-1364-9 (ePub)
Library of Congress Control Number: 2022914096

All Scripture quotations, unless otherwise indicated, are taken from the New King James Version®. Copyright © 1990 by Thomas Nelson. Used by permission. All rights reserved.

All Scripture quotations marked (KJV) are taken from the King James Version®. Public domain.

Dedicated to the memory of my big sis Marsha. Miss you. Love you. Can't wait to see you in the Morning!

"[B]ehold, I will pour out my spirit unto you, I will make known my words unto you."

Proverbs 1:23, KJV

Contents

Conversation 1: Christ and Christ Alone   9
   O Holy Night 2.0   9
   Crucifixion: The Nails, The Cross, Your Sins   12
   Sola Scriptura Then, Now, and Forevermore!   15
   Bread of Life   23
   Simon Of Cyrene—*It's Not That He Was Weak*   25
   The Garden Trilogy … *Three gardens, three trees, life eternally*   28
   Jesus is the Light of the World   42
   Mother Forgive Them …   52

Conversation 2: Dedication and Consecration   57
   A Prayer for Your People   57
   Baby Dedication Poem   61
   D.A.D. (Dedicated and Determined)   63
   Manhood Vows—Consecration of Young Men   65

Conversation 3: Love and Marriage   67
   Our Love 'Pilgrim'age   67
   CAME KNOCKING   72
   The Real Thing—A Marital Message for Millennials   74

Conversation 4: In the World But Not of the World   79
   Love Lifted the Prodigal   79
   Marching to Zion   82
   What Is … Men's Ministry   85

The Sins of the Father	87
You Could …	92
Grace, Grace, Grace (Grace to the 3rd Power—Father, Spirit, and Son)	95
God First	99

CONVERSATION 1

Christ and Christ Alone

Christmas music speaks to me on another level. I love the artistry and creativity used to paint the picture of an event that none of the writers witnessed but all believe occurred. I've seen paintings of scenes from World War I based on descriptions given to artists by eyewitnesses of the battles. Christmas carols like "O Holy Night" endeavor to do the same. However, the songwriter's task of lyrically recreating the scene of the most awesome event in the history of our world is a daunting task to say the least. I decided to challenge myself by using the poetic genre of spoken word/slam poetry to create a fresh rendition of a classic carol, and to express how I feel when thinking of the remarkable occurrence of the birth of God's only Son.

O Holy Night 2.0

O Holy night

O night divine, o night sublime

Night that altered history's timeline and redefined the existence of humankind

Within the confines of my feeble mind this biblical storyline feels surreal and difficult to deal with as genuine

I try to combine faith with vision to envision with spiritual precision what that night must have been like, looked like, felt like, with the dim light in the manger

providing the humble backdrop for the birth of the Savior

Gospel choirs of angels robed in heavenly apparel

Serenading sleepless shepherds with the sounds of the first Christmas carols

Perfect pitch and harmony to tell humanity that it has been saved from eternal peril

The night breeze rustles leaves up high in trees

While attendees of this miraculous occasion fall to their knees

Worshipping the Christ Child laying meek and mild in Mary's arms

The King of all kings delivered in a lowly barn resembling those found on peasant farms

O Holy night

The night of our dear Savior's birth

Bringing peace to earth, a gift beyond measure of worth

I see proud parents fussing over their heaven-sent infant

Whose arrival has ensured mankind's survival in an instant

How do you mother the Messiah, father the Prince of Peace?

Raise a son who will someday stun the world by walking on water and returning life to the deceased,

who will teach priests, figuratively feed sheep, defeat the beast by dying and rising like the sun does in the east?

At the very least, people will question this selection

Find it odd that God would choose these two to parent perfection

Mary, a pregnant unwed teen, Joseph a brother from Nazareth

A place where bad and evil connect, like major streets intersect

But on that night divine none of that had any relevance

God's understanding supersedes our simple levels of intelligence

So, the baby sleeps sweetly because He's in the good hands

of two ordinary people willing to submit to the Father's plans

O Holy night

The stars are brightly shining

And I'm slowly finding my way to Him

To worship the One who will lead a life without sin

A spiritual journey to the site of the Nativity

A place where I gain a true sense of my need for mercy and fall to my knees
The Creator being cradled, starting life as a helpless baby just for me
From Bethlehem to Calvary, from adoration to agony
Honestly, I wonder if I'll ever grasp the significance of that night divine
That silent night that ultimately saved this sinful soul of mine

I believe that art can be used as a vehicle to explore things that make us uncomfortable, are difficult to understand, or that we feel we may have heard or seen too many times to be interested. The cross and the significance of what Christ did for us at Calvary may fit under all of the aforementioned. Every year my local church uses the Easter weekend as an opportunity to do serious evangelistic work. Through a major dramatic presentation, singing, and spoken word, audiences comprised of people from the community and church members grapple with the complexities of the ultimate sacrifice. This piece was written for one of my church's annual Easter presentations. It is a short litany, otherwise known as Reader's Theatre, to be read or said from memory by three dynamic speakers. Timing, intonation, and syncopation help to bring color and strengthen the meaning of the piece. The nails, the cross, and our sins are personified in an effort to look at these vital elements of the crucifixion from a creative and fresh perspective.

Crucifixion: The Nails, The Cross, Your Sins

Speaker 1: Piercing, pointed, painful, pounded into His flesh
   Pushing past skin, veins, and nerves on my quest
   to render Him helpless and stuck
   Struck with force, I endorse the excruciating agony that my most venerable, now vulnerable victim feels
   Stainless steel, stained with the blood that seals the deal that was made back in Eden
   Puncturing the holy hands that helped to form man from dust
   Wretched, ranging four to eight inches in length, and prone to rust
   I am the nails

Speaker 2: Huge, hard, heavy, hostile, and horrific
   Intended use and purpose specific
   I am erected to slay the dejected
   Roman Empire instrument of punishment and doom, last stop before the tomb
   Passengers endure a splinter-riddled ride up high, pride tossed aside, exposed to many onlookers for miles and miles
   Piles and piles of dead bodies thanks to me

Most famous casualty slain at Mount Calvary

Stretched His arms out trans-continentally, pinned against me, creating a living poster of Grace and Mercy

I am cut, shaped, and fashioned from ordinary trees that were, ironically, created by Him

I am the cross

Speaker 3: Torn inwardly, born into me, created enmity between offspring instantly

I am the reason that you can't stop cheating, stealing, or lying, despite valiantly trying

To list all that I've done would take an eternity

I am the reason some of you will be lost eternally

You can commit me verbally or wordlessly, urgently or nervously, cluelessly or purposefully, but I come with a price, I'm never free

My wages are death, but you still find me attractive

You were warned about how I would tempt you and torment you, but you refuse to be proactive

What's happening to Him should be happening to you

The fate meant for you is what He's going through

You survive, He suffers and dies

I am your sin

Speaker 1: The nails

Speaker 2: The cross

Speaker 3: Your sin

All: Crucifixion!

Speaker 1: I had a role

Speaker 2: Played my part

Speaker 3: Did my job

All: Crucifixion!

Speaker 1: Do you really understand?

Speaker 2: Why it had to happen?

Speaker 3: How it changed everything forever?

Speaker 1: And yet you trivialize it

Speaker 2: Commodify it

Speaker 3: Commercialize it

Speaker 1: Turn it into something to hang at the end of a string, some beads, or gold links around your neck

Speaker 2: Or to sink with ink into your skin in the form of fashionable tattoos emblazoned on your backs or chests

Speaker 3: Superficial symbols—it's way more complex

Speaker 1: It's the apex of sacrifice

Speaker 2: An invite to paradise

Speaker 3: Redemption unfathomable, exemption unthinkable, and intervention inconceivable

All: Crucifixion

Speaker 1: The nails

Speaker 2: The cross

Speaker 3: Your sins

All: Forgiven

The Protestant Reformation was arguably the most impactful movement in world history. Its leaders and the ideology they espoused challenged, changed, and shaped both religious and secular institutions globally. For the 500-year anniversary of the reformation, the conference to which my local church belongs asked me to write a piece that focused on one of the tenets of Martin Luther's message. The piece was performed at camp meeting which is a collective gathering of all of the churches in the conference attended by over 7,000 people. It is written as a fusion of both Reader's Theatre and Chamber Theatre where vocal intonation and vocal dynamics enable the dramatic presentation to come to life with little or no props.

Sola Scriptura **Then, Now, and Forevermore!**

Speaker 1: He is a heretic!

Speaker 2: A lunatic!

Speaker 3: Death to him should be sure and quick

Speaker 4: Can you imagine this simple son of a miner questioning the undeniable, infallible, unflappable authority of …

All: (*clear throats*) The Roman Catholic Church?

Speaker 1: The storied history

Speaker 2: The awe and mystery

Speaker 1: The invincibility

Speaker 3: How could he

Speaker 4: Think for a minute

Speaker 3: Or even a second

Speaker 4: That he was in any position to be challenging or second-guessing

All: (*clear throats*) The Roman Catholic Church

Martin Luther: "Who knows if God has not chosen and called me, and if they ought not to fear that, by despising me, they despise God Himself? … God never selected as a prophet either the high priest or any other great personage; but ordinarily He chose low and despised men .... I am sure of this, that the word of God is with me, and that it is not with them."[1]

Speaker 1: He didn't like what he saw at the time

Speaker 2: And he had every right to be upset

Speaker 3: Burning with righteous indignation

Speaker 1: Same old, age-old corruption

Speaker 4: In every township, province, state, and nation

Speaker 2: Within Christendom

Speaker 3: Divine instruction and wisdom was ignored, exchanged, and replaced with the self-serving face of a leadership masking self-interest with false benevolence

Speaker 1: Hiding and perverting truth, leaving believers with no option but to follow false doctrine

All: Purgatory!

Speaker 1: Sounds familiar, but what exactly is it?

All: Purgatory!

Speaker 2: Ummm—it's a place, I think, but does it actually exist?

All: Purgatory!

Speaker 3: Is a place, according to Catholic theology, that serves as a holding station for souls after death. When in purgatory, souls must suffer and are tortured as they are purified and made fit to enter the kingdom of heaven.

Speaker 4: Over 500 years ago, Roman Catholic leaders told their followers that regular donations to the church could enable them to bypass purgatory, or could shorten the length of a dead relative's stay in purgatory. These donations were known as indulgences.

---

[1] Ellen G. White, *The Great Controversy* (Mountain View, CA: Pacific Press, 1911), pp. 142–143.

Martin Luther: Indulgences! I had no tolerance for this practice whatsoever! It was a scam endorsed and enforced by the church for over two centuries before I was even born. But in my time, this terrible custom had hit an all-time low. You see, my boss, Pope Leo, was desperately in need of funds to build a new cathedral to be named after saint Peter in Rome. He sent out Catholic clergymen to fleece his flock in order to build a most opulent structure that would bring praise to whom praise was due—himself, of course. Some of the clergy became a little too zealous in their efforts and would stop at nothing to swindle every last coin out of their poor parishioners. One despicable fellow, a monk named Johann Tetzel, even came up with a sleazy slogan! He would actually say, "As soon as the coin in the money box rings, the soul from purgatory springs." Ahh! He was a crook and a bad poet! Either way, after watching him manipulate God's people and watching the church continue to spread false doctrine, bending and contorting the Word of God, I could not remain silent.[2]

Speaker 1: 95 Theses

Speaker 2: Nailed to the door of the biggest megachurch in all of Wittenberg, Germany

Speaker 3: For everyone to see

Speaker 4: An invitation actually

Speaker 3: An opportunity

Speaker 2: To have a scholarly discussion, also known as a debate

Speaker 4: The topic …

> **After watching him manipulate God's people and watching the church continue to spread false doctrine, bending and contorting the Word of God, I could not remain silent.**

Speaker 1: Be it resolved that salvation cannot be earned through good deeds and works

Speaker 2: Cannot be purchased with a debit, credit, Visa, Amex, or MasterCard

---

[2] Ibid., pp. 127–128.

Speaker 3: Cannot be attained by swiping, sliding, tapping, or typing in your pin

Speaker 4: Cannot be bought with cold hard cash, a check, or a bribe

Speaker 1: No, no, no! Luther cried,

All: *Sola fide*!!

Speaker 2: Which simply means

Speaker 3: Faith alone

Speaker 4: Grants the sinner justification,

Speaker 2: Redemption, and ultimately, salvation

Martin Luther: Romans 1:17 says, "For in it the righteousness of God is revealed from faith to faith; as it is written, 'The just shall live by faith.'" After reading that, which follows Romans 1:16 which is all about salvation, how could I think otherwise? Faith alone makes someone just and fulfills the law. Faith is that which brings the Holy Spirit through the merits of Christ. It is a gift from God, and a living, bold trust in God's grace, so certain of God's favor that it would risk death 1,000 times trusting in it.

Speaker 1: Luther did risk death

Speaker 2: For saying what he believed

Speaker 3: And ongoing death threats

Speaker 4: For refusing to concede

Speaker 1: The 95 Theses

Speaker 2: Not initially created to be a manifesto

Speaker 3: But from the get-go

Speaker 4: Thanks to Johann Gutenberg's newly invented printing press

Speaker 1: Word started to spread

Speaker 2: No social media or internet?

Speaker 3: No need to fret

Speaker 4: Because when God has a message for His people

Speaker 3: He doesn't need WhatsApp, Snapchat, Instagram,

Speaker 2: Facebook, or fast and furious fake news feeds or trumped-up continuous tweets on Twitter

Speaker 1: To make sure that His truth will be delivered

Speaker 4: And that truth, that undeniable

Speaker 1 and 3: Undisputable

Speaker 2 and 4: Irrefutable

All: Truth

Speaker 4: Came from one source

Speaker 1: Not from political leaders or monarchy

Speaker 2: Not from the bishops, monks, or others who twisted meaning and made mockery

Speaker 3: Not from nuns, priests, professors, special advisors, or even the pope

Speaker 4: Martin Luther believed that none of the above could authoritatively, honestly, or explicitly express the blessed hope

Speaker 1: Like the Word of God

Speaker 2: The B-I-B-L-E

Speaker 3: The Scripture alone

All: *Sola Scriptura*

Martin Luther: The true rule is this—God's Word shall establish articles of faith, and no one else, not even an angel, can do so

Speaker 4: And as opposition to the truth steadily rose, Luther told believers to

Martin Luther: Pray not for me, but for the Word of God … Christ will give me His Spirit to overcome these ministers of error

Speaker 1: By the year 1520, Martin Luther's message founded in Scripture alone had become a threat to the so-called infallible rule of the papacy like nothing before it ever had

Speaker 2: Initially, he was seen by the Catholic leadership as a joke,

Speaker 3: A fly-by-night phony

Speaker 4: Why, even Pope Leo X dismissively referred to him as "some drunken German who will amend his ways when he sobers up."[3]

Speaker 1: But standing alone on the Word of God

Speaker 2: Martin defied the odds

Speaker 3: And shook the seemingly unshakable Church of Rome at its core

Speaker 4: And it finally realized that it could no longer ignore

Speaker 1: This meager monk turned professor

Speaker 2: Turned harbinger and radical, reforming messenger

Speaker 3: So, pairing itself with German emperor Charles V's legislature

Speaker 4: Church and state summoned Luther to appear before the Diet of Worms, a national assembly

Speaker 1: In order to strongly suggest that he think things over

Speaker 2: Realize the error of his ways

Speaker 3: Change his mind and his words

Speaker 4: And if he did, they'd try to forget what they had heard

Speaker 1: And maybe, just maybe, they'd let him live

Speaker 2: Leave him alone

Speaker 4: Let bygones be bygones

All: So, come on Martin!

Speaker 1 and 3: Do the right thing

Speaker 2 and 4: And stay in the land of the living

Speaker 3: Think about this carefully

---

[3] Jackson J. Spielvogel, *Western Civilization: A Brief History*, vol. 1 (Boston, MA: Cengage Learning, 2016).

Speaker 4: Say what we want you to say and be on your way home

Speaker 1: Remember what happened to those who went before you like Jerome?

Speaker 2: Or even poor old John Huss?

Speaker 3: Who stubbornly stuck to his beliefs, was burned to death and whose ashes were thrown into the Rhine, settling on top of the water like specks of dust

Speaker 4: So, Martin you must

All: (*loud whisper*) Hush!

Speaker 1: Because you know

Speaker 3: What happens to those

Speaker 2: That go against us, so

All: Hush!

Martin Luther:
> "Since your most serene majesty and your high mightiness require from me a clear, simple, and precise answer, I will give you one, and it is this: I cannot submit my faith either to the pope or to the councils, because it is clear as the day that they have frequently erred and contradicted each other. Unless therefore I am convinced by the testimony of Scripture or by the clearest reasoning, unless I am persuaded by means of the passages I have quoted, and unless they thus render my conscience bound by the word of God, I cannot and I will not retract, for it is unsafe for a Christian to speak against his conscience. Here I stand, I can do no other; may God help me."[4]

Speaker 4: And with that, Luther would inspire people the world over to read the Scripture closer and know God's Word better

Speaker 1: Prayerfully examining every book, chapter, verse, epistle, or letter

Speaker 2: From this sprung the Calvinists who believe in irresistible grace, and the perseverance of the saints

---
[4] Ibid., p. 160.

Speaker 3: The Anabaptists who preached and reached many with the message of adult baptism

Speaker 4: The Methodists who spoke of God's allowance of free will concerning our rejection or acceptance of His salvation

Speaker 2: Many others like the Congregationalists, the Pentecostals, Quakers, Episcopalians, the Baptists

Speaker 1: And eventually, in 1863, the Seventh-day Adventists

Speaker 3: Whose emphasis

Speaker 4: On the three angels' message, the seventh-day Sabbath

Speaker 2: And the blessed hope of the return of our Lord and Savior Jesus Christ continues to ignite the flame of reformation

Speaker 1: Author Ellen G. White says that the reformation did not end with Luther[5]

Speaker 3: And that new light has been continually shining upon the Scriptures, and new truths have been constantly unfolding

Speaker 4: The reformers started what we've been called to finish

Speaker 2: Our efforts, our hope, our faith cannot diminish

Speaker 1: We must study, fast, and pray, stay in the narrow way, never give up or give in because we're almost home

Speaker 3: And keep our minds and our message rooted and cemented in God's Word

All: *Sola Scriptura*, Scripture alone

---

[5] Ellen G. White, *The Great Controversy* (Mountain View, CA: Pacific Press, 1911), p. 148.

I have found that life has disappointed me in many ways when I search for worldly satisfaction. Validation, popularity, and flattery can only satisfy you for a moment and leave you feeling extremely empty in the long term. Jesus told us through imagery when He likened Himself to water when speaking to the woman at the well, and by comparing His truth to bread, that He is really the only One that can truly satisfy our needs. Jesus' use of imagery and personification were so effective that I decided to take the same approach in this piece to describe just how fulfilling a life centered on Him can be. Our insatiable appetites for things that can harm us can only lead to destruction, when a simple diet of the Living Water and the Bread of Life can lead to everlasting satisfaction.

Bread of Life

I am—not what you see on shelves of grocery stores in different varieties silently trying to convince buyers that I am more nutritious and delicious than other brands

I am—not limited or restricted to a short shelf life indicated and communicated by expiry dates printed on a tag hanging around my neck

I am—not to be buttered, battered, French toasted, grilled with cheese, or roasted and grated into crumbs

I am—not even the unleavened brand broken and served at Communion—for that is just a symbol; what I tell you is complex and at the same time simple

I am not made from whole wheat, but I am Most Holy

I had twelve disciples not twelve grains,

I tried to explain—in John 6:35 but people then and now think too literally, lacking the figurative yeast to spiritually rise and comprehend what could be understood by the least

Are you hungry? Well, here I am.

I am the Bread of Life

You said you were hungry; you appear to be hungry

Indulging in slice after slice of sin

Belly full but still starving for peace within

I am the Bread of Life

I am above and below when you serve me—forming a *sanctified* sandwich

Average consumers have great debates over whether I am better brown or white

But those who have tasted and have seen how good I am don't care as much about my color, they are happy to be precious in My sight

Are you still hungry? No need to be hungry. Why are your cupboards bare when I am right here?

With Me your daily bread is sure

I can feed you till you want no more

> **Are you hungry? Well, here I am.**
> **I am the Bread of Life**

I am the Bread of Life. I am the Bread of Life. I am the Bread of Life.

If pictures speak 1,000 words, then most of the pictures that we see of Jesus would resoundingly state that He was probably one of the weakest and physically frail individuals to ever walk the earth. In an effort to capture His meek and gentle demeanor, He is often depicted in illustrations and dramatic presentations as being exceedingly delicate and fragile. I personally feel like nothing could be further from the truth. Examples such as the authority with which He spoke, the trade that He learned and practiced, and His ability to command respect from even the elements of nature give me the image of a powerful man whose understanding of the most powerful and purest emotion that one could possess, being love, made Him also the most approachable and desirable person to ever live. When asked by the director of my church's annual Easter play to represent Simon of Cyrene in a spoken word piece, I wanted to make it unmistakably clear that Simon was not asked to carry the cross because Jesus was the weakling that we often see in pictorial and dramatic presentations. Simon had a role to play, just as the Roman soldiers and others who were present at the time did. It was a small but very significant role. It should add to our understanding of just how devastating and immensely difficult Christ's mission and suffering was, but it should by no means bolster or act as justification for the narrative of a weak and fragile man in need of a savior when He was, in fact, the one and only Savior of the world.

Simon Of Cyrene—*It's Not That He Was Weak*

It's not that He was weak, or that I was so strong

These pictures painted of Him looking frail while being sainted have got it all wrong

You see, this was a carpenter who rolled with rough and tumble fishermen, can you picture them

following some lowly, little, lightweight? There's been a mistake,

or at least a misconception, correction must be made,

I was told to carry the cross, and I obeyed

But it's not that He was weak, or that I was so strong, I mean, come on

This was the same Man who was able to turn over tables and chase those crazy moneychangers out of town

On that day, He said what He had to say, and none of them tried to take Him down

So, it's not that He was so weak, or that I was so strong

What I'm saying is, I was just there standing, gazing,

Soon to be part of a scene that this simple Simon of Cyrene never dreamed he'd partake in

Roman soldiers calling me out, I was sure they were mistaken

What about Peter, Judas, and His other ten men, or was He now totally forsaken?

Visibly shaken, now making my way towards Him who is without sin—our gaze connects and injects within me a new respect

For in this moment, I realize that this is the Son of God whom they reject, violently flog, and disrespect

While I, the one whom they select, approach humbly and circumspect

In retrospect, I must once more stress that—

It's not that He was weak, or that I was so strong

My bio in the Bible may be short, but that walk to Golgotha was dreadfully long,

The unrelenting tormenting continued as we slowly pressed on,

It probably hurts even worse when you know you've done no wrong

I tried to remain calm, silently recited the 23rd Psalm, but the Shepherd in that verse is the One they now curse

Romans, Jews, men, and women of every nationality, shouting, showering Him with piercing profanity,

As He prepared to give His life for every hue in humanity, even the average Afro-Asiatic like me

See, it's not that He was so weak or that I was so strong

Bearing the sins of mankind is beyond any mortal muscle or brawn

He was tired, abused, beaten, heartbroken but hardly speaking, profusely bleeding but still proceeding,

Up the high, haunting, harrowing hill called Calvary with me leading

Grieving my position, unworthy of such a mission,

I served with no volition, but gained a new conviction

While I witnessed the incisions through His hands, side, and feet,

I might have carried His cross but realized that I was weak

Yes, I am weak, but He is strong

These are more than just the words to a popular children's song,

I for one, could not resist the temptation, to call 10,000 angels to end the situation,

Snatch me off the cross and show them right then and there who was the King of all nations,

And that is why I could only bear the weight of the wood and not the world

Because it's not that He was weak or that I was so strong, and of course, He knew this was true all along.

The whole plan of salvation begins, is fulfilled, and concludes in a garden setting. Our sin in the Garden of Eden, Christ's surrender to His Father's will in the Garden of Gethsemane, and eternal life in the Garden of Eden restored in heaven are ultimately the three most impactful events in human history. The Garden Trilogy is an Easter play that endeavors to recreate the events and situations that occurred in these most important locations. It includes flashbacks and flash-forwards stemming from Christ's conversation with the angel sent from heaven to encourage Him as He agonized in the Garden of Gethsemane prior to His crucifixion. I wanted to show how tightly connected everything is that happens in each location with particular emphasis on what I feel the angel sent to speak words of encouragement would have had to say in order to give Him the strength, motivation, and power to complete the most difficult task ever faced by anyone in history. What could one say to encourage the other to take on the weight of every evil act ever committed on earth and to be punished as if He were guilty of it all when, in actuality, He had never even come close to ever doing anything wrong? Prayer and the sanctified influence of the Holy Spirit gave me the opportunity and the courage to explore the inexplicable in this short dramatic presentation.

The Garden Trilogy ... *Three gardens, three trees, life eternally*

Act 1, Scene 1
Interpretive dance to the song "The Garden"[6] by Kari Jobe. A YouTube lyric video should be on the screen *(dancers are in the Garden of Gethsemane dancing to a portion of this song before the actors come out)*

Act 1, Scene 2—Gethsemane
Jesus and the disciples are walking slowly together toward Gethsemane. While they are talking, He starts to stumble, and the disciples reach out to hold Him up. They realize that something is seriously wrong and they start to ask questions in an effort to figure out what's happening. (Garden and nighttime sounds—crickets chirping, a breeze blowing, leaves/bushes rustling, etc.)

John: Master, what's wrong? You don't look well at all.

---

[6] Kari Jobe, "The Garden" official lyric video, YouTube, https://1ref.us/1sg (accessed January 10, 2022).

James: Are we walking too fast? I know I'm still full from our Passover feast. (*Looking at the others*) Maybe we need to slow down. We can even stop and rest if you want to.

Peter: Yeah, let's sit down. Teacher, we can sit here for a bit until You feel better.

John: Yeah, let's sit

James: I could go for a nap right now

Peter: Yes, brother, I'm gonna take my sandals off, kick back, and unwind

Jesus: (*Says laboriously, gasping, heavy voice*) No, no. You-you stay here. I need some alone time with My Father. I'll just be over there.

John: Look at Your face, Master! You shouldn't go any farther. Sit down and I'll go get some water—

Jesus: No! (*gasps, then softly*) You stay here and pray. Please.

Peter: Lord, can You fill us in on what's going on here? What's happening to You? I've never seen You like this before!

Jesus: It's-It's My soul, Peter. I've never felt this feeling before. I-I feel like, like, like

James: Like what, Master?

Jesus: (*In a dry, hoarse, forceful yet desperate whisper*) Like death! Like death. You three—Peter, James, my beloved John. You are My closest friends. You're My brothers. That's why I asked you three to come away with Me without the others. I need you to stay here and pray for Me while I go and talk to our Father. Please. Don't stop praying until I return. Can you do that for Me?

Peter: Yes, Master

James: For sure

John: We will do anything for You

Jesus stumbles away from them and eventually falls on His face. Hearing the disciples gasp and start to come toward Him, He quickly raises His hand, indicating that they should stop. They go back and sit/kneel and begin to pray in hushed tones, slightly audible.

Jesus: (*Loudly, with His face still buried for the first few words, and then slowly rising to His knees*) Abba! Abba! Father! (*Softer, as He rises to His knees*) My Father. My Father. (*Slowly, and tearfully, shaking, trying to muster strength to make this request*) Father. (*Deep breath*) Oh, My Father, if it is possible, let this cup pass from Me (*pause, deep breath, somewhat tearfully*); nevertheless, not as I will, but as You will. Father. (*Feeling the separation from the Father, yells in desperation*) Father! Abba! (*Falls on His face again*).

Slowly gets up to His feet. Staggers back to the disciples for some support.

Jesus: Peter! James! John! (*Almost in disbelief*) Were you sleeping?

Peter: (*Groggy*) Sorry, Master-I-I just shut my eyes and—

James: I saw Peter taking a break, so I thought that it was okay—

John: I'm sorry, Lord. I drifted off without realizing it—

Peter: Teacher, Your face! If it wasn't for Your voice I don't know if I'd believe that it's You. You look different.

John: Master, I'm starting to become afraid. How can we help You? (*The others vocally agree with John*)

Jesus: Please, calm down. The best way that you can help Me right now is to pray for Me. Stay awake and pray. The evil one is busy. He is always busy, but he is working extra hard right now, so stay awake and pray that you do not fall under his control. Your hearts are willing, but the flesh … the reality is, you are very weak. Without the Father's help you are weak. So stay awake and pray. I will be back.

Peter: Master, where are You going?

James: Why are You leaving again?

John: Let us come with You

Jesus motions for them to stay, He stumbles off, bent under the load of sin, back to His spot to pray again.

Jesus: (*On His knees, almost panting*) Oh, My Father, if this cup cannot pass away from Me unless I drink it, Your will be done.

Flash of light representing lightning and a rumble of thunder is seen and heard as the angel sent from heaven (Luke 22:43) appears in the garden.

Song: "He's the One"[7] *by Deliverance is sung, preferably by the angel (only the two verses and chorus, then fade out). Jesus is on His knees, face buried, praying and agonizing while the song is being sung.*

When the song is finished, the angel speaks and Jesus realizes that he is there.

Angel: Jesus, Son of Man, Emmanuel, God with us, Son of the living God, I have been sent by the Father, Your Father, to strengthen You, and to let You know that You will have the victory.

Jesus: (*Gasping, but slowly becoming calmer, looks heavenward and loudly whispers*) Thank You, Father. (*Then looking at the angel*) The evil one, he tempts Me. He tells Me that if I bear the sins of this fallen race … (*pauses, trying to calm Himself further, to catch His breath*) he tells Me that if I bear the sins of the world, I will be separated from the Father forever. He tells Me that this cannot work. He tells Me that the Father and I will never be one again.

> The evil one is busy. He is always busy, but he is working extra hard right now

Angel: He is a deceiver and the greatest of liars! You are feeling separation from the Father because He cannot bear to see You enshrouded by sin. But You will be with Him again. The evil one is hitting Your humanity with all of his might, but You must focus on why You were sent, on why You left all of glory. You are in the Garden of Gethsemane now, but what happened in the Garden of Eden is the true reason why You are here to redeem, to save, and restore ….

Jesus: (*Still slightly breathless*) Eden, yes, yes. The Garden of Eden, and the tree (*gasps*) of knowledge of good and evil. Disobedience. Sin (*falls forward, exhausted*).

Lights fade to complete darkness

Act 2, Scene 1—Garden of Eden
Lights up. Garden of Eden, pleasant garden sounds—babbling brook, birds chirping, etc.

---

[7] Deliverance, "He's the One," *Say You Believe*, Tyscot Records (1986), download at https://1ref.us/1sh (accessed January 10, 2022).

*Adam enters as music for **"I Come to the Garden Alone"**[8] starts. Song is sung preferably by Adam (only the first two verses and choruses). Second verse, Jesus joins Adam in the garden. They walk as the song continues, enjoying the surroundings of the garden together. The song finishes.*

Adam: Is it time, Lord?

Jesus: Yes, it is, Adam. Are you excited?

Adam: I think so. I mean, I don't really know what to expect.

Jesus: Do you trust Us, Adam?

Adam: I do, Lord.

Jesus: Perfect. (*Huge smile*) We know that you will be very pleased, Adam. Just lie down right here and before you know it, it'll be all over, and life as you've known it thus far will never be the same again.

Adam: Lord, You are so awesome. You made all of this for me to enjoy. And to think that there is still more yet to come is simply incredible! (*Embraces Jesus*) So, You want me to lie down right here?

Jesus: Right here is just fine, Adam.

Adam lays down and Jesus kneels over him. The sounds of a breeze getting stronger and stronger is heard representing the presence of God the Father and God the Holy Spirit. The lights start to dim gradually until completely black. The sound of the strong breeze is still heard. When the lights come back on, Eve is seen on the opposite side of the garden to where Adam is laying down. The breeze starts to fade and Adam wakes up. He looks across at Eve in total wonder and amazement. She starts to walk over to him slowly as he starts to speak.

Adam: I'm awake, but it feels like I'm still dreaming ….
Eyes not believing what they're seeing
The Father escorts you over to me and gently places your hand in mine
Fingers intertwine, perfect design
Body, spirit, and mind—united
Excited—as we, the first two members of humankind
turn to each other and embrace

---

[8] C. Austin Miles, "In the Garden," 1913, https://1ref.us/1si (accessed November 1, 2021).

I see eternity in your face
Bone of my bone, flesh of my flesh and altogether lovely
Created by Him to be loved by me
The mommy to be of all earthly progeny
One rib plus three
Father, Son, and Holy Spirit ingenuity
Intricately created my counterpart
Truly a heavenly work of art
Lord, how great Thou art
And how beautiful is she
My Eve, my queen, my s-o-u-l-m-a-t-e (*word spelled out, then said by Adam, whispered by Eve*), soulmate.

Eve: Look at my man.
Shaped and sculpted by God's hands
Perfection from inception, divine invention, no correction necessary
Priest of our Edenic sanctuary
My extraordinarily cute contemporary
and I are literally made for each other
Each day we will uncover—
a new passion for life with one another
Brother is naked and not ashamed
In a union that God ordained
Totally holy
I love me some him
And he is certainly into me
Flawless symmetry, stimulated intellectually
We connect on the highest level—both physically and mentally.

Jesus enters, overjoyed, happy to see the couple together and getting to know each other. The music for **I Come to the Garden Alone** *plays as Jesus and the couple stroll through the garden. He takes them to the tree of knowledge of good and evil, He points to it and the audience sees Him explaining (wordlessly and through gestures) that they can eat from all of the other trees in the garden except for this tree. They nod, showing that they understand, and after embracing them again, He leaves them. Adam and Eve walk away from the tree to look around the garden.*

Eve: So, you named all of the animals?

Adam: Every last one of them.

Eve: Even the Rhinocerusususis?

Adam: It's pronounced Rhinoceros, my love. And yes, I named them too. I tried to get a little creative on that one. You don't think I got too carried away, do you?

Eve: Rhinoceros. No, I think it's perfect!

Adam: Thank you!

Eve: Oh, Adam, I just love everything about this place!

Adam: Me too! Isn't the Lord wonderful? He made all of this for us to enjoy, and then to top it all off, He made us for each other.

Eve: Oh yes, He did! (*Gives Adam a hug*)

Adam: Hey, Eve, let's water these plants over here and then go for a swim.

Eve: Sounds good to me.

The two start watering the plants. Eve becomes distracted.

Eve: Adam, what's this?

Adam: It's called a butterfly, Eve.

Eve: It's gorgeous! I wonder where it's going.

*Eve follows the butterfly. Adam is oblivious and continues watering the plant. Eve ends up beside the forbidden tree. (**Don't You Touch That Tree** by Lisa McClendon[9] is sung live or played while this transpires) She stops suddenly as if she's heard her name being called. She looks at the tree and a light coming from the tree attracts her to it. She starts carrying on a short inaudible conversation through gestures and facial expressions. A breeze sound effect is heard as Eve takes the fruit from the tree and starts to eat.*

The breeze sound effect becomes louder, more intense. Adam senses something is wrong and looks over in the direction of the forbidden tree. He is mortified. He goes over to ask Eve what she's done. Through inaudible conversation

---

[9] Lisa McClendon, "Don't You Touch That Tree," Gracelyrics, https://1ref.us/1sj (accessed January 10, 2022).

and gestures, she convinces him to eat the fruit. The breeze gets louder and the lights flash on and off to indicate that all has gone wrong. Adam and Eve look around the garden frantically and finally go and crouch in a spot in an effort to hide. The breeze dies down but is still heard softly. The lights stop flashing and a voice is heard over the breeze.

God (*Off stage*) **Adam, My son. Where are you?**

Adam: (*Stuttering, afraid*) I-I-I heard Your voice in the garden, Lord, and I was afraid, so I hid myself.

God: Afraid? Why would you be afraid, son?

Adam: Well, because I-I'm-I'm naked.

God: Adam, who told you that you were naked? (*Pause, as if waiting for an answer*) Adam, have you eaten from the tree that I commanded you not to eat from? I told you not to do this from the very beginning and I was very clear. You were told that you could eat from any tree in the garden. Any tree, Adam. It was all for you. I asked you to stay away from only one tree, and I told you what would happen if you ate from it. Oh, My son, what did you do?

Adam: (*Trying to think of an excuse or find something to say*) I—Lord, I know—it was the woman, the one that You put here in the garden with me. She gave me some of the fruit from the tree and … (*pause, disappointed in himself*) I ate it.

God: Eve, My daughter, what is this that you have done?

Eve: (*Looks over at Adam and they both look at each other helplessly*) Lord, it was the serpent. It tricked me and I ate. I believed what it said to me and now—(*voice breaks as though she is about to cry*).

Jesus reenters with animal skins for them to wear.

Jesus: (*Handing them the clothing*) These are for you. You will need to wear them from now on as the temperature will no longer be perfect and you will need to protect your bodies.

Adam: Lord, these are the skins of animals. Did these come from …? I don't understand. How did You make these? How did You remove these from the animal without—

Jesus: That is the price of disobedience, Adam. Sin. The wages of sin is death. We told you this. And We told you because We love you. We wanted you to understand that you had and will always have the opportunity to choose to obey or disobey. But with every choice there are consequences.

Eve: So, what we did has caused the animal from whom this skin was taken to—

Jesus: Die. To die. As all that is alive will eventually die. But there is a plan. A plan to erase what has happened here today and to save you and the generations to come.

Adam: Thank you, Lord.

Eve: We love you, Lord.

Together: (*Weeping*) We're sorry!

Both fall on Jesus weeping and He embraces them.

Lights down

Act 3, Scene 1—Gethsemane
*One minute of interpretive dance to Kari Jobe's "**The Garden.**"[10] Song fades and Jesus, the disciples, and the angel resume their positions—disciples in a position of prayer soon to fall asleep again, and Jesus in conversation with the angel.*

Angel: The sins of Adam and Eve and every human after them must be atoned for through the ultimate sacrifice. Death was wrought by the eating of the fruit which hung from the forbidden tree and now life will come from You being hung on Calvary's tree. (*Points to the cross. Hopefully it will be in view, maybe on the screen?*)

Jesus: I know. I know what I must do. But this weight, this separation from My Father, this evil that is sin, it all feels like too much. It feels like it's permanent. Like it will last forever.

Angel: It will not. Remember when You said, "Destroy this temple and in three days I will raise it up"? You knew then that death nor the grave could ever hold You down and this is still true! You are the Son of the mighty God. You are the Prince of Peace and the conquering Lion of Judah. You will die but You will rise again!

---

[10] Kari Jobe, "The Garden," https://1ref.us/1sg (accessed January 10, 2022).

Jesus: (*Pulling Himself together, getting stronger, and slowly taking on a more upright position*) I came to erase the first Adam's mistake. I came to die so that all might have life, and have it more abundantly.

Angel: Yes! Amen! And think about this abundant life that they will have because of You. You saw Eden lost, but Yeshua, Deliverer, Son of God and Son of Man, think about life for all humankind in Eden restored! Think about life for the good and faithful in the garden in heaven!

Jesus: Heaven. The tree of life. Heaven.

Judas and the Roman soldiers enter the garden. The disciples wake up, looking around, surprised and confused. Judas greets Jesus with a kiss and the Roman soldiers advance toward Him to arrest Him. Lights fade to black.

Intermission

Act 3, Scene 2—Heaven, Garden of Eden Restored
*Song: "**The Garden**"[11] by BeBe and CeCe Winans is being sung, with the words scrolling on the screen. Angels represented by the dancers are there in white moving to the song. Adam and Eve (dressed in white) enter after the first verse and chorus. They are looking at the garden restored, looking at their surroundings, contemplatively and joyously at the same time. They see Jesus coming toward them and they fall at His feet. He stoops down and pulls them up and takes them deeper into the garden (by the second chorus of the song). The song ends and Jesus speaks.*

Jesus: Adam. Together again in a perfect place. Never to be separated. Eve, mother of all humans. Welcome home.

Adam: Lord, I want to say so much right now, but I can't find the words. Eden is more beautiful, more magnificent—I mean, how did You improve on perfection?

Eve: Lord God, I thank You for Your mercy and for Your grace. Like Adam said, Lord, I—(*shakes her head in awe and thanksgiving*) I can say nothing that will truly express how I feel to be here again. I—

---

[11] BeBe and CeCe Winans, "The Garden," 2009, https://1ref.us/1sk (accessed November 1, 2021).

Jesus: I know, Eve. And I am overjoyed to see you two here, together with Us for all eternity! So, you like what We've done with the place, do you? (*Stretches His arms out, and Adam notices the nail prints in His hands.*)

Adam: (*Taking hold of Jesus' hand*) My Lord, what is this?

Eve: (*Taking hold of His other hand*) It's on this hand too! Was this part of the plan?

Jesus nods His head slowly.

Adam: Lord, can we know more about the plan? You told us that we would know more about it, that we would understand it by and by. Tell us, Lord, what exactly did You do? How much did You suffer?

Jesus: Oh, Adam, it wasn't easy. It really wasn't. But it was worth it.

*Music for **"Mary Did You Know"**[12] starts playing. Downstage, Mary is seen with Joseph, holding the baby Jesus. They are speaking inaudibly, smiling at the baby and each other. When the singing of the song starts, they freeze in tableau until the song ends.*

Eve: Lord, we want to know more. Can You tell us, show us the plan? How did it happen?

Jesus: Well, I came to earth as a baby. Born to a teenaged virgin.

Adam: You're kidding!

Jesus: Oh, it's the truth. Have a seat. We have eternity for me to tell you all about what happened in thirty-three years. You see, I ….

His voice trails off as the singing of the song starts but He continues to tell the story of His life to Adam and Eve. He pantomimes (or a separate set of actors downstage pantomime) different parts of His life, showing them how He grew up (reasoning and reading in the temple and working as a carpenter with His father), and His years of ministry (calling the disciples, being baptized, turning water to wine, walking on water, calming the storm, casting out demons, healing the blind, lame, lepers, raising Lazarus, feeding

---

[12] Pentatonix, "Mary, Did You Know?" official music video, YouTube, https://1ref.us/1sl (accessed January 10, 2022).

5000+, debating with Pharisees, etc.), while Adam and Eve listen to/watch Him (or them) and react until the song is over.

Adam: My Lord! You did all of those amazing things while You were on earth? The people must have adored You!

Eve: Well, of course they did! You were healing them, teaching them the truth, and showing them the Father's love. They must've followed You everywhere, all night and day!

Jesus: They all recognized that there was something special about Me, but not all were pleased with Me or eager to be in My presence. You see, the same one that deceived you way back in the first Eden continued to deceive your offspring for centuries and millennia. He tricked some of them into thinking that I was a false prophet, a troublemaker and rebel intending to break the law rather than fulfill it. Many chose to believe his lies and accused Me of blasphemy. They refused to see Me as the Messiah. Satan convinced them that My work and My words were so offensive that I deserved to be put to death. (*Music for* **Calvary** *by Richard Smallwood starts to play softly*) And while giving My life was the only way for the human race to be freed from a debt that they could never repay, the evil one made sure that My death would be the cruelest, gruesome, and most painful experience that anyone would ever endure.

Jesus motions for them to look in the direction of where the voices of the mob yelling, "Crucify Him" are coming from. He exits the stage at the rear. Lightning and thunder effects. Shouts of "Crucify Him" get louder.

Act 3, Scene 2—Crucifixion
Jesus slowly walking toward the stage, carrying the cross with the Roman soldiers and the mob behind Him, yelling at Him and beating Him.

Calvary *by Richard Smallwood is sung while Jesus is walking and carrying the cross, and while He is being hung on it. While He is walking, being hung, and the song is being sung, snippets (recorded voice-overs) of events that happened leading up to the cross are heard "Greetings, Rabbi" (kiss), "I find no fault in Him," "Give us Barabbas," "I swear, I don't know the man" (rooster crow).*

Song is finished. Immediately after song stops ...

Jesus: (*Loudly*) It is finished! (*Thunder sound effects and light flashes for a lightning and thunder effect.*)

*He is lowered and taken off of the cross while the instrumental music for **Calvary** continues. After He is taken out, Adam and Eve come downstage, front and center in the spotlight, to address the audience.*

Both: This is our story
Adam: This is my story
Eve: This your story
Both: This is <u>the</u> *("the" is pronounced with the long E sound)* story
Adam: of humanity
Eve: the creation
Adam: the damnation
Eve: the victory
Adam: Three gardens
Both: Three trees

Eve: Paradise lost, the cost of disobedience spawned from curiosity
I walked with him *(points to Adam/touches Adam)* and Him *(points heavenward or to the cross)* in the garden that I was living in
I was cautioned constantly about the tree that was forbidden—
But you can hear and not listen, I believed my place in perfection was a given
Made the choice to ignore the voice of my Lord for the temporary joy of materialism
And in my mistake, I would inadvertently create a template for the "holier than thou" mindset or the sitting-in-the-back-pew, hypocritical, Christian who believes that salvation and heaven's admission is theirs because they follow doctrine and practice religion.

Adam: Make no mistake, our mistake is your mistake
We made ours early, but think about the ones you've made lately
Think about the serpents that you allow to distract you and lead you to sin daily
Human frailty is real, the devil knows our weaknesses and he appeals
to every one of them openly and subtly
conniving, contriving, crafting cruel capers cunningly
He got to her *(points to Eve)*, to you and to me, and that's why I thank my Lord for that tree on Mount Calvary
I wasn't there, I didn't see, but He told me that He had a plan and with my whole heart I believed

He suffered excruciating, insane pain in the Garden of Gethsemane
Being tortured by the enemy to save a wretch like me
Amidst an atmosphere of gloom, He was buried in a tomb, but He rose on day three
And ascended into heaven in front of men from Galilee
And in heaven—there is a tree
With fruit that's sweeter than the sweetest pineapple, Julie mango, cherry, *soursop, guinep, chenet, or ackee
It's called the tree of life and we can eat from it every day, all day, freely and eternally (*music for* **Back to Eden** *by Donald Lawrence starts*)
So, believe in the Father, believe in the Son, and believe in the Holy Spirit, the blessed Trinity
Let everyone within the hearing of my voice, every man, woman, boy, and girl
Surrender your life to Him, and you will enter into the new Eden, and literally live life on top of the world!

Song: *"Back II Eden"*[13] *by Donald Lawrence is sung*
Entire cast comes out to dance, sing, and show the joy of life in Eden restored.

The End

*soursop, guinep, chenet, ackee—fruits that are exclusive to tropical climates such as the Caribbean (may be called by different names from island to island and in other regions of the world).

---

[13] Donald Lawrence, "Back II Eden," https://1ref.us/1sm (accessed November 1, 2021).

Jesus is the Light of the World is written as a blending of two genres, namely slam poetry/spoken word and Reader's Theatre. The piece was written for a Christmas cantata. The idea was to utilize song and spoken word to examine earth's history through a biblical lens with an emphasis on the need for Christ to come, depart, and come again. I decided to use the approach of having the audience serve as a class of students in a lecture hall with the performers in role as the professor and teaching assistants to heighten engagement. Each "lesson" in the piece alluded to different songs to be performed by various groups, soloists, and choirs, providing a unique method of introduction. The underlined and bolded words are meant to be emphasized and to help the speaker understand the unorthodox rhyme scheme.

Jesus is the Light of the World

Lesson 1—Intro and Creation

Professor: Good morning, class. Today's topic in **question** should make for a most fascinating and intriguing **lesson**

iPads, Chromebooks, MacBooks, laptops, pens and papers, or whatever notetaking <u>device you like</u> should be fired up and ready to record this lyrical, spiritual **session**

I'm **guessin'** many of you will be familiar with the <u>content</u> but <u>time spent</u> in *review* will bring *new* **blessings** so before I <u>proceed</u>, I will <u>need</u> your full and undivided **attention**

Which means no texting, WhatsApping, DMing, <u>Snapchatting</u>, because I can see you in <u>the back and</u>—

Help <u>me</u> 'cause I will lose it if I catch you taking <u>a selfie</u> while I'm **teaching** so please show some respect while I'm up here **speaking**

With help from the <u>brilliance</u> of my esteemed teaching <u>assistants</u> (*all reach into their pockets and put on eyeglasses at the same time or some action that displays that they are all in sync*) we will use the disciplines of history,

Teaching Assistant 1: Anthropology

Teaching Assistant 2: Social Science

Prof: and eschatology to examine the origin of our existence, our present state of subsistence

TA 1: and life in the unforeseeable distance

TA 2: also known as

TA 1 & 2: the future.

Prof: Men and women, boys and girls
No washroom breaks, sit up straight as we investigate today's topic—

All: Jesus the Light of the World.

Prof: History will be the first discipline that we use to examine this terrestrial ball that we call planet earth before and just after the arrival of sin

TA 2: The definition of history

TA 1: is simply

TA 1 & 2: A branch of knowledge that records and explains past events

Prof: And while experts and professionals in the field have spent exorbitant amounts of time compiling primary and secondary sources

TA 2: We have found that when compared to other historical textbooks

TA 1: the Bible is the most reliable of all sources

Prof: So, in spite of all of the popular prolific scientific hypotheses and philosophies and unfounded resolutions like the Big Bang Theory and Charles Darwin's Evolution

Today we will defer to the Word of God to bring the great debate concerning Creation to its conclusion

No disrespect or no *offence* to anyone in the *audience* who may believe that you and me

are the proud *descendants* of a microscopic organism that decided to grow arms and legs after floating around in the sea

Or that we should be inviting orangutans, gorillas, and monkeys to our family get-togethers and parties

But hardly any of these so-called schools of thought that we are taught will ever endeavor to explain the inner workings of the human brain

TA 1: Why we are rational beings

TA 2: Dealing with morals and emotions like joy and pain

Prof: In order to obtain the answers to questions that I'm sure everyone in this class has asked

we, your esteemed educators, grappled with the best way to approach this. And after much deep dialogue and deliberation the consensus is that we give our undivided attention to God's lecture on the topic found in the book of Genesis

TA 1: Genesis?

TA 2: Genesis?

All: Genesis!

> **We have found that when compared to other historical textbooks the Bible is the most reliable of all sources**

Lesson 2—The Fall

Prof: So, God made man, human beings, and being in His image, He beheld them, took a good look at them and saw that they were good

TA 2: Real good

TA 1: Everything nice

TA 2: Just right

Prof: No enmity, no fights, no strife

TA 1: Just the Creator watching a perfect husband and wife living the best life

TA 2: No sunscreen needed for the warm rays on sunny days,

TA 1: clothed in nothing but righteous light

Prof: Accepting invites to spend nights strolling through the garden with the Father by moonlight

TA 2: Perfectly physically proportioned in stature and height

TA 1: Given dominion over everything in sight,

Prof: Eating delicious, delectable delights until—

TA 2: Until?

TA 1: Until …

All: That fateful bite

Prof: The slippery tongued serpent, the incorrigible brute tempted Eve with more than just fruit

More than just the sweet juice, seeds, stem, and skin. He tempted her with power, a haughty pride that resides deep inside, leading the first earthly mother to sin

All: Listen, students!

Prof: This is the height of social and cultural anthropology

An event that would forever alter our behavior and biology

Adam and Eve grieved the loss from their error and its cost and in terror looked at each other and the serpent and started to play the blame game

Passing the buck with no luck because they were stuck and we, humanity, would never be the same

TA 1: Our lives are shorter

TA 2: Days are hotter, nights are colder

Prof: Weakness from diseases increases as we grow older

We turn a blind eye, turn our backs, refuse to look over our shoulder

At people being bullied, abused, or killed as criminals grow bolder

The entry of sin in the Garden of Eden was a turning point, the ultimate game changer

TA 1: But God had a plan for fallen man in the form of a Redeemer, a Savior

TA 2: His Son, the Everlasting One, the Prince of Peace, His Co-Creator

TA 1: Would humble Himself to be born to a pregnant teen from the "hood" in a manger

Prof: Nothing seems stranger to a world wrapped up in the elements of commercial Christmas

When in actuality, there's nothing greater than the redemption His birth would give us

In a little town called Bethlehem

surrounded by His parents, animals, shepherds, and eventually wise men

Mary's little sacrificial Lamb was born, and from a boy to a man, would grow to be the King of kings and the Lord of lords

TA 2: A great teacher, a healer of sons and daughters

TA 1: A miracle worker, a leader, a water walker

Prof: Our life story's author, shaping, molding, making, recreating us like clay in the hands of a potter

TA 1: Wow! Can you imagine being in Mary's place and looking into the face of your Deliverer as He's being delivered from your womb?

TA 2: Giving life to the Life-giver, the One who would save you from an eternal tomb?

Prof: Yes, Mary had a little Lamb who would save sinful man and rightfully command respect and praise from all creatures here below

but as she nursed this child with a tender smile, one has to wonder,

All: did she really know?

Lesson 3—His Death

TA 1: After living thirty-three years of a sinless life

TA 2: Emmanuel, Yeshua, Jesus the Christ

Prof: had reached the apex of His ministry

But before it was finished, He

gathered His disciples together in the upper room to explain

what to the unbeliever would seem insane.

The reason why He came and what He had left to do

What He was about to go through

needed clarification so that they would no longer misconstrue the real purpose of His mission

and prepare those eleven Jews to become the first Christians

The incisions that would soon pierce His hands, side, and feet

were a by-product of the Godhead's decision to make our salvation complete

TA 2: The wages of sin is death and the only pardon that we could receive for our mistake in the garden—

TA 1: would be the shedding of innocent blood from paradise, a sacrifice that would be the ultimate display of love

Prof: Captive Israel was looking for a political savior

A king seeking glory on earth, who would punish their enemies for their behavior

Conversely Christ came to seek the lost at all cost

Creating controversy culminating in a cruel death on Calvary's cross

He would exhaust all accusations made in the attempted assassination of God's character which claimed

that we serve Him out of fear to keep His severe wrath and anger tamed

So, Mary's Lamb would eventually be captured, tortured, and slain

Enduring humiliation, blood-filled perspiration for the exoneration of my guilt and shame

TA 1: To clear my name!

TA 2: To cleanse my stains!

TA 1: The Lamb was slain

TA 2: And from His veins

Prof: poured the blood

TA 1: Oh, the blood

TA 2: Nothing but the blood

Prof: That soul-cleansing fountain blood

TA 1: That reaches-the-highest-mountain blood

TA 2: That flows-to-the-lowest-valley blood

Prof: That saving-thieves, murderers, adulterers, and-drug-addicts-in-the-back-alley blood

TA 1: That redeeming blood

TA 2: That down-from-Calvary streaming blood

Prof: That blood that will never lose its power

Class

Students

Sinners

Saints

All: Pray to be washed in that blood this very hour

Lesson 4—The Resurrection

TA 1: Okay, class

We're moving fast

TA 2: And we hope you've been paying attention

Prof: We've covered roughly 4,000 years of history through a social-scientific-meets-spiritual lens to broaden our limited dimensions

TA 1: We have mentioned
Our creation

TA 2: Our fall

Our Savior's birth

Prof: His sinless life and subsequent rejection

But for some, this section may be the most challenging part of the lesson

Wrapping our finite minds around the reality of His resurrection

Here's a quick question

How many of you have used your textbook recently?

Coming to lecture, taking the occasional note won't be enough for the final exam. You need to study frequently

Nonetheless, I digress, but if you have your book on your smart device or in hardcopy, then turn with me

Either John chapter 20 or Matthew 28. While you search, we can wait

It's Sunday

Day three

And we find a weeping Mary, distraught and teary-eyed
Feeling lonely and hopeless as she cried

TA 1: No sign of the Master
In her mind a clear disaster

TA 2: But before long were spoken the words
Probably the sweetest she'd ever heard

Prof: The angel of the Lord appeared
Begged her not to be scared
And told her in no uncertain terms, "He is not here"
The same Jesus of Nazareth, who many believed had breathed His last breath
Completed His conquest and after a short rest, now stood all glorious and victorious over death

TA 2: Astounding!

TA 1: The highest display of His magnificence!

Prof: However, class, some of you will probably ask
What is the significance?
The resurrection of our Lord Jesus Christ confirmed His identity
Who else can raise themselves from the dead?

TA 1: Not many

TA 2: Not a few

All: Not any

Prof: Before Him, great teachers had been listened to and obeyed
Other miracles had been displayed
Other prophets had prophesied
But none could restore their own lives
Not even if they tried
Any who comes in the last days proclaiming to be the Messiah,
performing so-called miracles is deranged, delusional, strange, and odd

Jesus' life, death, and especially His resurrection means

All: He is the true Son of God

Lesson 5—The Second Coming

TA 1: The lesson is just about over

We're at the end of today's class

TA 2: And I'm pretty sure that some of you are silently saying, "Free at last!"

Prof: But the conclusion of the lesson contains the biggest blessing

and in some ways, it's the foundation upon which everything else that we said is resting

Interesting to see that once a year a few of us will care to hear the story of His birth

The amazing and miraculous, attracting us to regale in the tale of how Jesus arrived on earth.

Before His resurrection and ascension, however, the Lord made a promise that should relieve believers of all tension

In John 14, He made mention of His intention to return for the collection of His people—those who remained faithful

To take us home to freely roam the streets of the New Jerusalem and to claim our seats at the welcome table

This is not a fable or a story; He is able, and He will surely come in the same manner that He left

Without a doubt His coming is sooner than we like to preach about or speak about, and we should be excited to see what's next

So, it's time for dismissal, not just from class but soon from this world of mass destruction

TA 1: Mass corruption

TA 2: Mass consumption

All: Perpetual evil, misery, and woe

Prof: I can't wait to sit at the feet of Jesus

And hear Him unfold this universe's purpose like a thesis

Students

Classmates

Brethren

All: Let's all be ready to go

After watching different newscasts and reading different accounts of the initial incidents and subsequent protests of the shootings of unarmed young men in various parts of the United States, it made me think about a few things. As a new father, it made me think about the pain that the parents of the victims were experiencing. Watching the protests and seeing people of all ethnic backgrounds coming together to speak against injustice made me think about how the desire to be treated with dignity is a common human want and right. Finally, it made me think about the audacity of forgiveness—the peculiar act of communicating that you hold no malice or evil desire in your heart toward someone who committed some great or small deed of wrongdoing against you that is causing you gut-wrenching agony. Jesus asked His Father to forgive the individuals who were killing Him while they were in the middle of carrying out the act. His mother watched His murderers, and probably heard Him utter these words. Hearing her Son ask His Father to forgive them must have inspired her to do the same. I used this piece to inspire us all to believe that we are capable of forgiveness because of His amazing example. The mothers in this short Reader's Theatre piece are as follows: Sybrina Fulton is the mother of Trayvon Martin. Trayvon Martin was shot and killed by George Zimmerman on February 26, 2012, in Sanford, Florida. Zimmerman was a self-appointed neighborhood watchman who believed Martin was a potential threat to the community. Lesley McSpadden (some sources have her last name listed as McFadden) is the mother of Michael Brown. Michael Brown was shot by a police officer, Darren Wilson, on his way home from a convenience store in Ferguson, Missouri. The shooting of the unarmed 18-year-old took place on August 9, 2014. Finally, Gwen Carr is the mother of Eric Garner. Garner was killed by a police officer who used a chokehold during his arrest. The chokehold used by the officer was said to be prohibited. Garner died on July 17, 2014, in New York City.

Mother Forgive Them ...

Male voice (MV) (voice of Jesus): Mother, forgive them for they know not what they do

Sybrina Fulton: You wore a hoody

Lesley McFadden: You had your hands up

Gwen Carr: You couldn't breathe

Mary: You didn't say a mumbling word

MV: Mother, forgive them

Sybrina: I love you

Lesley: I miss you

Gwen: I still grieve you

Mary: I always believed in You

MV: Mother, forgive them

Sybrina: I want to, but it's so hard

Living, existing in a world that's been marred

by sin

hatred external and within

The pain I feel, I want to heal, but how do I begin?

To understand all of this, make sense out of madness

hold it together, be eloquent and intelligent in front of story-hungry savages

Cell phone, Skittles, iced tea, gated community, hoody, suspect, male, black

Media buzzwords, twisted facts and stats that altogether lack

The tears and silent prayers of a mourning mother who just wants her baby back

It's been three years,

my son is gone and I'm still here,

dealing with personal anguish plus public perception, emotion and varied opinion

Lord, I need answers, signs, relief, but all I hear is …

MV: Mother, forgive them

Lesley: I'm trying to, but it's not easy

Hearing people speak for or against your son on TV, radio, or social media freely

can cut deep; I lose sleep, and still weep, believe me

From anonymity in small town Ferguson, Missouri,

to countrywide controversy

Anderson Cooper asking what I think of the grand jury

and struggling with why my son's life ended early

Peaceful protestors, looters, and violence

Long nights when I suffer in silence

Were his hands up? Are the police corrupt? Did he act in defiance or total compliance?

Reliance on an alliance between the police and my community is a suggested solution

But for my son's death I need soul-healing restitution and resolution

Confusion and civil unrest threaten to get the best of me

Acquittal and lost life urge me to act aggressively

Lord, I need strength, mercy, comfort, and wisdom

On my knees begging for these, but all I hear is ...

MV: Mother, forgive them

Gwen: I need to, but how do I start?

When seeing the video of how he spent his last moments alive breaks my heart

Falling apart with each replay, watching his lips form the final words that he would say

"I can't breathe"

And with that he would leave

A city, a nation, maybe a planet, divided

System decided, no officer indicted

Protest ignited, and pain uninvited now resides with me

Speeches delivered passionately about a man, forty-three, with a family,

New Yorkers and athletes united behind a slogan on signs and t-shirts actively

trying to make deadly wrongs right

But few know what it's like to see your son beg for his life

I saw them wrestle my boy to the ground

Until his body lay limp lifeless left in a mound
Nothing more than dirt on the skin of the Big Apple
Daily I grapple with the desire to love in the face of hate
Not to hope for my son's executioners to suffer a similar fate
And have their mothers, lovers, and children outlive them
And feel what I feel, but I hear You pleading ...

MV: Mother, forgive them

Mary: I did, and it made all the difference
But it took a lot, especially because of His undeniable innocence
Ever since conception, misconceptions, labels, stigmas, and stereotypes would follow my Son for the duration of His life
Pregnant, teenage mother, not yet wed, living in the hood
Some people missed the blessing, busy second-guessing if Nazareth could produce any good
Sanctified suspect, ostracized reject, exemplified perfect, crucified blameless
Enduring a replayed recording is gut-wrenching, but I was an eyewitness
to the height of human sickness, beating, torturing, killing my Boy who they all knew was sinless
But amidst the gravest injustice stood His message of forgiveness
He said to do it seventy times seven for those who sin against us
He was betrayed with a kiss, beaten with whips and fists
And in the end, He prayed for all those who were involved in this
His trial had more flaws than the "stand your ground" laws
And eventually, He would end up with His hands up and outstretched
As He too struggled for breath before death
His last sentence was a whisper, but I could still hear it
"Father, into Your hands I commit My Spirit"
Learn from my Son as I did
Look in His face and feel fear, pain, and anguish diminish

Sybrina: Stand your ground

Lesley: Hands up

Gwen: I can't breathe

All: Hatred

MV: It is finished

Mary: Because He loves them

All: We can forgive them. To Him, our lives matter

> **Learn from my Son as I did**
> **Look in His face and feel fear,**
> **pain, and anguish diminish**

CONVERSATION 2

Dedication and Consecration

Intercessory prayer is arguably the most powerful and humbling opportunity that we have. Standing in the gap for a loved one or even a stranger is a privilege that we should never take lightly. When I was asked to offer a prayer on behalf of my church family during our main worship service, I was honored and overwhelmed. I had heard individuals pray on behalf of the congregation many times before, but I did not feel like I could find the right words to make a strong enough, or a spiritually rich enough appeal to the King of kings that could truly represent the desires and needs of over 1,000 people. I prayed about it and asked the Lord to help me to present this prayer to Him in a way that would be a blessing to those who heard it and to myself as I presented it. I also asked that it would be satisfying to those who were earnestly in need of someone to petition our God on their behalf, and that it would be pleasing to Him as the words ascended to His throne. I asked the individuals who requested that I do the prayer if it would be acceptable if I presented it in the form of a poem and they said that it would. I asked my cousin to play the hymn Is Your All on the Altar, and to end with a slower rendering of When We All Get to Heaven on the piano while I prayed. At the end of the prayer, I was shocked to see tears flowing and people silently and audibly giving God the praise that only He deserves.

A Prayer for Your People
Lord, we all long for sweet peace and
for our faith to increase
So today we earnestly and fervently pray
Realizing that we can't have true rest, or be perfectly blessed,

until our all on the altar of sacrifice is laid.
So, as we kneel before Your awesome throne
And acknowledge that You are God and God alone
while the Holy Spirit moans and groans in intercessory translation,
I offer this simple, solemn, and sincere supplication
on behalf of our lowly, humble, and submissive congregation.

And who am I to be given this great task?
Innumerable are my sins in this week just passed
But, Father God, You are a better forgiver than I am a sinner, and that's fortunate for me
So, while others reject me, You always accept me "Just as I am, without one plea"
And as sure as Christ our Savior and King in heaven intercedes
Father, I know that You'll look beyond my faults today, and see our multiple needs.

Your children have come forward for many different reasons,
wants, and desires that vary and change like seasons,
Mere mortal weaklings, plagued by sinful legions
Gathered here believing that our God will grant us healing—
So, Lord, send Your healing, for if there's one thing that we believe and know
There is a balm in Gilead to heal our sin-sick souls

And with this faith we present our sick and our shut-ins
Both those who have been long-suffering and those who have fallen ill all of a sudden
Wasn't it You, O Lord, who said, "If My people, which are called by My name would humble themselves and pray then I would hear from heaven"?
Then in humble obedience we beseech Your omniscience, and expect no less than a miraculous medical blessing to be extended, and diseases and illnesses ended, for many of our infirmed brethren.

Requesting divine medicine also for those whose problems are mental, spiritual, social, economic, and emotional

Praise You, God, for being a listening friend,
and while ruling the universe, still being approachable

And now, righteous and noble Father, I present to You our church holistically
Worshippers everywhere, far and near, Christ's body
Adorned and blessed with love, talents, and diversity
Purposefully positioned in place for a time such as now
Endow us, Father, with a spirit of unity
From the young to the elderly—let us be
Cognizant of the fact that we're fighting the same enemy
Help us to readily fall in line and face the foe side by side
Eradicating jealousy, envy, and pride, because we need each other to survive
Please bless our leaders, officers, elders, and administration
and our pastors, Lord, who shepherd this congregation
Bless our seniors, dear Father, without them we couldn't function
Encourage us to give a keen ear to their wisdom and instruction—
Provide strength and forbearance for those among
us who are parents
because it's not easy to raise a child against the grain
of the devil's interference

We also present our young adults and teenagers to
You in dedication
Set them aside in consecration to exemplify Your will
to this generation
And as our more experienced members endeavor to admonish
them concerning all that is evil and corrupt,
Constantly remind us that as saints, we were all once sinners who
fell down, but through grace have gotten up

And finally, Lord, as we observe the world and all that's going on
the wars, the hurricanes, the earthquakes, we know
now it won't be long
With all the crime and corruption
municipal and federal leaders scrambling to correct social wrongs
And as the evil one persuades millions that all hope is gone

We who have read and heard Your Word take courage
and remain strong
Believing that soon we will shout the glad song—
Christ returneth hallelujah, hallelujah, amen
The reunion of loved ones, of family, and friends
An eternity to spend with You, Lord, the One who
loves us the most
Hearing or singing the song of Moses and the Lamb in the
presence of the heavenly host
When we all get to heaven, what a day of rejoicing that will be
O even now, Lord Jesus, we pray for You to come quickly
But until then, Lord, keep us faithful, and help us
to fight the good fight
In the name of the Father, the Son, and the Holy Spirit
May the words of our mouths and the meditations of our hearts be
acceptable in Thy sight
Amen and Amen

The birth of my older sister's daughter was a special occasion. Her daughter would be the first girl child born to one of the five siblings in our family. For some reason, her birth made me start thinking more seriously about what it would be like to be a parent myself. I thought about all of the unsaid expectations and desires that new parents and family members have for newborns and how oblivious they are to all of the excitement they cause. When my sister told me that she wanted me to participate in the blessing of her child, I wanted to make sure that I represented the family well. Her child was the first grandchild to be born after my mother passed away, and my mother was a huge believer in the important role and responsibility that parents have in a child's salvation. I wanted to make sure that I emphasized that the baby's dedication, much like a wedding, is only one day, but what happens afterward is what really counts. Bringing your child to the Lord is step one in the journey toward eternity.

Baby Dedication Poem

I've heard it said that a child is a promise, that each child is a possibility
Lying there innocently while parents, friends, and family
fuss, fondle, and fawn, going on and on
about
recognizing characteristics or traits of some great ancestor that can be
seen in the way the child smiles or moves her head, but only anticipating being fed
this little one is totally oblivious to all that's being said
Unaware of the dreams that are being dreamt on her behalf
of the sincere wishes and hopes that she chooses the right path
of the fact that she can send her mommy and
daddy into delirium with just the sound of her laugh
unable even to possess the enormity of this occasion
within her mental grasp
And as we gasp in sheer wonder and amazement over
every new development and stride that she makes,
we must also pause to thank God for the miracle
that occurs every morning when she awakes
See this demonstration of parental supplication where

dedicatory orations are delivered by good ministers is
not merely a show, but on the contrary it's a necessity—
To combat the evil one who attacks from day one
we come on bended knee requesting earnestly and fervently
that you will "lead her my God to Thee"
Honestly speaking, could you conceive our existence
or being without God's divine protection?
Though television talk shows with so-called
psychological pros spread this "power within" misconception—
God bless the child whose parents recognize that they need a spiritual connection
from the tenderest age, helping them to turn a
Bible page and embodying Christlike affection—
Before your inception, before you entered this world
and immediately captured this entire family's undivided attention,
before your earthly father's first adoring kiss
or your mother's first wise and loving words of comfort or correction
Before the name Rianna was ever typed, written, or mentioned

God the Creator knew you and loved you
Anointed you in your preexistence and placed none other above you
So, we pray that you will "early seek the savior"
yearning and learning to shine your little light,
With this smiling collective of friends, cousins,
siblings, aunts, uncles, parents, and grandparents
supporting your every move, baby girl—
I just know that everything's gonna be all right.

> **And as we gasp in sheer wonder and amazement over every new development and stride that she makes, we must also pause to thank God for the miracle that occurs every morning when she awakes**

Being a father has been the most exciting, frightening, and challenging experience of my life. It has highlighted my strengths, exposed my weaknesses, strengthened my faith, heightened my fears, and filled me with more love than I ever thought I was capable of producing. Written for a Father's Day celebration, this poem expresses what I have learned and what I strive to accomplish with regard to the all-important role of "D.A.D."

D.A.D. (Dedicated and Determined)

What can a father offer a child that's unique?

Can he bring anything that can compete with a mother's kiss on the cheek?

What can a father offer that's exclusive?

That a mommy and a mommy's child won't find intrusive

Can't give birth or breastfeed—best believe those are out of the question

Biological activities activating an immediate maternal connection

Plus, misconceptions that pit masculine and affection as polar opposites

What can a father offer in the midst of all of this?

Well for starters as the first man in his daughter's life

A father can exemplify how a husband should treat a wife

And break this critical, cyclical phenomenon

of women with skewed views on relationships, seeing proverbial bad boys or fixer-uppers as soulmates and then wondering what went wrong

A father with a strong, noble and Christlike character,

Can enhance his daughter's chances of living happily ever after

After-dinner talks and Sunday afternoon walks help his kids to not see themselves as afterthoughts, but rather as Daddy's priority

Surely—still aware of his authority—but also delighting in his friendship.

The list of things a father can offer his children is endless

From day one a father can be a son's role model

Rearing and preparing him for a world that won't coddle, forgive, or make things easy

A father, not the army, can really teach a son to be all that he can be

Sending him into battle saddled with spiritual ammunition

Training him to stand like the brave and face the foe with no fears and inhibitions

A real caregiver of the paternal persuasion uses every occasion

To reflect on what a father can offer the next generation

Diligently manning his station as the head of the family

The manifestation of his love is worth more than what he earns annually

Daddies and daddies to be, approach your calling with pride, reverence, and dignity

And let the world see what every father should offer his God-given progeny

Love, love, and more love—from now until eternity

That's all a heavenly Father can ask an earthly father to offer.

The transition from adolescence to adulthood is becoming increasingly more difficult, particularly because society appears to be rebelling against it. From the promotion and endorsement of foolish stunts and pranks being carried out by individuals well into their adult years on social media and television, to airbrushed pictures and the insane pressure placed on men and women to attain and maintain unrealistic standards of physical appeal by the media, people are being encouraged to place "staying young" at the top of their priority list. My church has started a tradition of holding a "coming of age" ceremony for 16-year-old boys. Fathers, uncles, older brothers, and male role models selected by the boys attend the ceremony in a show of support for the young men and to encourage them to embrace their transition into manhood and the important responsibilities that come with it. I carefully and prayerfully created "Manhood Vows" at the request of the organizers of the consecration service that each young man agreed to uphold and to hold each other accountable to over the course of their individual manhood journeys.

Manhood Vows—Consecration of Young Men

1. Will you consult your heavenly Father concerning any and every decision that you make, knowing that you have access to wisdom that is far superior to any here on earth, while recognizing that God does not work according to our time and our demands but always for our good in that particular moment and the future?

2. Will you commit to taking responsibility for all of your actions, and refrain from using circumstances, influences, or past occurrences in your life as a scapegoat or a default excuse for poor decision-making, knowing and embracing the understanding that a man must be able to look himself in the mirror and hold himself accountable for every word spoken, for every transaction made, and even for every thought that he has allowed to enter and reside in his mind at the end of each day?

3. Will you always recognize the importance of being a role model for your peers and for the generations immediately following you and for generations yet to come, by embracing and cultivating positive attributes/characteristics, and acknowledging that a man's true strength should not be measured by his muscles, abs, height, and other

physical attributes, but rather by his ability to stand for up for justice, to seek peaceful solutions rather than violent ones, and to show love to everyone, even to those who will never offer love to him in return?

4. Will you always honor and cherish the women in your lives and show the utmost respect to every woman that you come in contact with, knowing that women are equal in ability and value to men, and thus, must never be taken advantage of, disrespected, disempowered, disregarded, or verbally or physically abused? Will you be careful to remember that God's intention and perfect plan was and still is for men and women to work with each other, bringing their equally unique strengths together in a united effort to build better homes, societies, and citizens under His supreme guidance?

5. Will you allow your leadership qualities to be a benefit and accessible to those in your church, family, community, and your place of employment, and will you make every effort to develop your leadership qualities even further by taking the time to seek the advice of your elders and put the counsel that they give you into action, by studying other leaders and trying to adopt some of their qualities and principles to your own life, by possessing a willingness to serve and give back to your community whenever the opportunity presents itself, by being a man of your word and always fulfilling your obligations?

CONVERSATION 3

Love and Marriage

This piece was written and performed on the wedding day of two dear friends whose family name happens to be Pilgrim. A pilgrim is a traveler, and a pilgrimage is a journey. The surname that the couple would soon share made me think about how a loving relationship that leads to a wedding and continues on in marriage is indeed a journey. In the piece, I tried to show the ups and downs and somewhat unpredictability of the journey. In spite of our greatest efforts to plan everything in order to have a perfect wedding day, and to plot the course of marriage, there will be, inevitably, some things that we just do not anticipate coming our way. It takes work, prayer, and then more work followed by more prayer. On the day of the wedding, the performance of the piece was accompanied by two actors who portrayed what was being said. It felt like the visual helped to make the words come to life and, in essence, become more real to the audience and hopefully to the couple. My desire was to show them that love can be awesome and challenging, but if it's truly ordained by God, it's all worth it.

Our Love 'Pilgrim'age

Male: I couldn't help but take notice of you

Female: And I took notice of you noticing me

M: Showing me something brand new, I wondered if you were indeed

Both: the one

M: The difference maker

F: My lonely-state emancipator

M: The *dime piece that would cause me to desist and cease my trivial pursuit of surface cute, magazine model bodies, and shallow-minded hotties

F: The sweet thing that would untie knotted heartstrings and unearth buried seedlings of feelings that I truly believed were doomed to never bloom

M: I'm looking at you

F: and you're looking at me

M: With the same expression

F: Silently asking the same question

M: Could you be

F: Really be

M: Truly be

Both: the one?

F: Holding hands strolling through the park or the mall

M: Playing hard in front of the boys, but checking my phone on the low to see if I missed your call

F: Playful tugs, followed by long, tight hugs

M: Flowers just because, my life is nothing like it was. Everything is going great!

F: (*With attitude*) But you were thirty minutes late!

M: You're going out with your girls again?

F: Are you gonna criticize me for every dollar I spend?

M: Why do you think you're always right?

F: Are you trying to start a fight?

M: Sometimes I wonder

F: sit there and ponder

M: start to question

F: start second-guessing

M: Is this God's will?

F: Are you still …

Both: the one?

M: This isn't the end, is it?

F: I'm not ready to quit

M: This isn't easy, but I believe that God is leading me

F: He's leading me

Both: Leading us

F: to trust Him, and to trust each other

M: to submit to His direction

F: to build a love the stuff of legends

M: to love all of your perfect imperfections

F: becoming best friends first, recognizing the best and the worst in each other's characters

M: minimizing surprises and shocks, giving this relationship a legitimate shot at "happily ever after"

F: A new day, a new chapter, writing our love story and submitting it to be edited by the Master

M: It's filled with plot twists that we couldn't predict: climaxes, authentic conflicts, and resolutions

F: sincere soul-searching for solutions, anticipating every episode and

M: committing to sticking it through to the conclusion

F: Taking it slow but not slowing down

M: Setting our own speed limit from start to finish

F: I'm more sure than I was before

M: I want you to feel secure. My intentions are pure

F: Questions are being answered, doubts are being displaced

M: fears are being erased, I'm seeing "forever" in your face

F: It really feels like you are

M: I believe that you are

F: I finally see that you are

M: I'm down on one knee because you are

Both: the one

F: A wedding

M: A marriage

F: A day unlike the average

M: A new beginning. What's in our future?

F: Maybe a big house, a vacation in Paris, and a baby carriage?

M: God knows, and time will tell, but today, I'm here to say "I do"

F: "I do" take you as my husband, my man

M: "I do" commit myself to my wife, my woman, and to His plan

F: "I do" to the ups and downs, the joys and sorrows

M: "I do" to the reality of today, and the unpredictability of tomorrow. "I do"

F: Baby, please say it again

M: "I do" because you're my best friend

F: "I do" because I love you

M: "I do" and I love you too

F: "I do" and now I know you are

M: forevermore you are

F: I thank the Lord you are

Both: The one

dime piece—contemporary slang meaning beautiful woman. A ten-cent piece of money is called a dime. A dime is equivalent to the number ten, and a beautiful woman is a perfect ten out of ten; she is a dime piece.

> **A new day, a new chapter, writing our love story and submitting it to be edited by the Master**

In today's world, couples get married for different reasons. Some marry to share the cost of living, almost like a business partnership. Others have "open marriages" where spouses are "allowed" to see other people while hoping to maintain some strange sense of security connected to the fact that they will always have someone to come home to when the outside relationships are no longer satisfying. I am still a believer in love being the best and only reason two individuals should enter into the intimate and sacred institution of marriage. I was asked by a couple that I really did not know to write a piece for their wedding. Since I couldn't make it personal, I thought that I would express my feelings about love and marriage being synonymous and personifying "love" to make it something that people could visualize and connect with.

CAME KNOCKING

True Love came knocking at our door and we answered it

Created a romance with it

Weathered every circumstance with it

Allowed our feelings and emotions to advance with it

then watched it flourish in the garden where God planted it

Forget the generic, we created our own brand of it

And now in the presence of family and friends we boldly take a stand for it

We have expectations we demand of it, and questions we still ask of it

But, today we pay tribute to its incandescent glow as we bask in it

You see, *it* is Love and Love is *it* and

if Love is sincere, then *it* never quits—

Through all the ups and downs, the happiness and hurt,

everything is secondary because love comes first

Yes, first comes love and then comes marriage

the all-important institution that distinguishes true love from the average—

True Love came knocking at our door and we stepped aside allowing it to enter

It looked around, made itself comfortable, and decided to stay forever

It is the best houseguest, relieving stress with tenderness

Replacing fair weather with faithfulness

Erasing traces of emptiness

Making intimate requests

Reminding us that we're blessed

Promising to remain the same in times of more and in less because

This Is Love,

Not to be mistaken with a fleeting adoration or momentary infatuation

This Is Love

The reason for our celebration, and the foundation of our unification

True Love came knocking at our door and we believe,

that its presence is the greatest gift that either of us could receive—and that is why—we let *it* in.

I find millennials to be fascinating. They champion new ways of thinking, frown on those who cling to old views and approaches but find it stylish and deem it cutting edge to celebrate anything that is considered a "throwback" or "retro." I find it fascinatingly intriguing that they can make oxymoron a point of view, and that they are able to brilliantly defend it and legitimize it. When a millennial couple that I absolutely adore asked me to write a piece for their wedding, I took this approach in my endeavor to explore a loving relationship and to offer some advice. Using the chorus of a song from a generation before my time as the foundation, I flavored the piece with things that are undeniably a part of the millennial reality. Recommending long established, tried and true principles to navigate through and contend with the challenges of our postmodern society was my best attempt at replicating the approach used by King Solomon in the book of Proverbs. The wisest man who ever lived encouraged us to make practical use of timeless spiritual wisdom, and I prayed that the Lord would use this piece in a similar way.

The Real Thing—A Marital Message for Millennials

Ain't nothing like the real thing, baby

Ain't nothing like the real thing

"Ain't Nothing Like the Real Thing" was a song and a catch phrase

but nowadays

trying to define the "real thing" can really bring the inquisitive mind to its proverbial knees

the position of a beggar, a borrower and not a lender, the receiver of an "I'm breaking up with you" Snapchat or WhatsApp message and not the sender

See, the so-called "real thing" is mediated and has been infiltrated by mixed messages containing only tiny vestiges of the truth

From back in the days of Dr. Ruth

to the golden era of Oprah to now in your top picks

on Netflix

The "real thing" is constantly being rebranded and repackaged

to appease and ease the average mind

into accepting everything and settling for a whole lot of nothing at the same time

The new "real thing" will tell you that on your wedding day—as long as you smile while looking into each other's eyes when you say "I do" at the start—

that you don't really need to take in or pay much attention to the "till death do us part" part

'Cause if you don't really like how things feel after the first few fights—

then you're well within your rights

to say that y'all are through, find somebody new and bring all of your Glad garbage bag baggage into their life

Trust me, you're good

I mean that's how they do it in Hollywood

Holding onto your marriage through misunderstandings, misconduct, miscarriages, money mismanagement is not something the new "real thing" believes should be understood

or even tolerated

Also hated by the new "real thing" would be

openness and honesty

Sharing cell phone lock codes and social media passwords is unheard of

simply because

I don't think I need to be upfront about everything that I do

or everyone that I talk to in order to prove that I love you

Listen, the fact that you've got me *booed up

should be more than enough

to let you know that you can trust me

and for what it's worth, don't think the worst if you hear my phone alerts every night around two or three a.m.

Pay them no mind, believe me, everything is just fine

Please understand that the new "real thing" is designed

to convey intimacy through emojis, bitmojis, private DMs and other superficial forms of screen time

Building oneness through constant deep, emotional, in person, personal conversations

is not necessary or even an obligation

according to the new "real thing" regulations

As a matter of fact, trying to crack carefully constructed cones of personal space is not viewed as love busting its way through but rather as an invasion of privacy violation

Sounds a little bit like an oxymoron, doesn't it?

Invading your spouse's privacy but the new real thing doesn't take this lightly

Not surprisingly, society often chooses to view love in certain communities

or amongst particular ethnicities as less legitimate or insignificant

Hurled into this western world and given a blueprint to follow, forced by the dominant culture to swallow pagan interpretations of the "real thing"

Valentine's Day, red hearts, a chubby creature with a bow and arrow and two wings

And measuring the strength of your love by the weight and the size of your rings

A few more things that will be held against you two is a long dirty laundry list of your ancestor's troubles in relationships since being forcibly removed from their home continent

Infidelity, a fractured emasculated mentality

"Your love cannot be the real thing," they will say, "just look at how your people behave on *Jerry Springer when four or five guys could potentially be one baby's daddy."

So, it is of no small consequence

that your lives, your future, your love will be up against

a plethora of barriers to prove that it is real

Indulge me as I steal a moment on your wedding day to convey what I feel in the form of a three-point charge or an appeal

Point number one:

As you look around and see others changing partners like socks, shoes, or hairdos

Purpose in your heart that this will never be you

Allow your marital vows to resonate in your mind, permeate your flesh, and bind you two together

Let your love control the weather

so that storm clouds such as arguments that may go on for hours are nothing more than passing showers and will not last forever

And remember, you've made this commitment in front of all of us, your loving family and friends to the end; if you break your bond you break our trust

And we do trust you

And we do love you

But we will *cuss you

If you don't follow through

Point number two:

Be totally honest with each other and be transparent

Be up front; let your actions and intentions be obvious and apparent

In marriage, secrecy is almost always synonymous with guilty—

Filthy habits and wrongdoings will surely come to light

Be BFFs and nothing less, be vulnerable, genuine and never let lies or pride leave you in a precarious plight

Finally, point number three:

Do not allow stereotypes and a media that loves to highlight our challenges both past and present to represent or define who you are as individuals or as a couple

Telling half-truths and whole lies and skewed stats that justify why in some people's eyes our relationships are destined for trouble

Burst their little prejudicial bubbles, destroy the myths—and any glass box that they try to stuff you in please ensure that it shatters

In a world that will try to disable you by labeling you I want you to show them that Black Love Matters

Be that example, that ample sample size that illuminates and illustrates exactly who you are

Be affectionate, hold hands, hug and kiss in public, and live your lives like shining stars

Ain't nothing like the real thing, baby, and when you've got it, there's no need to pretend

May the God of heaven bless you and keep you together forever and ever Amen.

booed up or boo'd up—to be in an exclusive romantic relationship.

*This is a reference to the exploitative, over-representation of African Americans taking paternity tests on shows such as Jerry Springer and Maury Povich to reveal the identity of the child's true father. Predictably, emotions run high and the guests often end up fighting, crying and getting into verbal and physical altercations with each other. These shows proliferate stereotypes and provide a one-dimensional representation of African American relationships. The popularity of the shows can be connected to their efforts to create perfect conditions for the most volatile situations and outcomes. The perpetuation of stereotypes can be far-reaching, and black people across the globe have felt the impact of being viewed and pre-judged based on what is seen on these shows.

cuss—in Caribbean culture the word "cuss" does not necessarily mean using curse words. "Cuss" primarily means to scold, verbally chastise, or tell someone off.

CONVERSATION 4

In the World But Not of the World

This piece was written for a church youth program titled The Ultimate Love. When I was thinking about the theme, I believe that the Holy Spirit led me to reflect on the parable of the prodigal son. The love shown by the father in this story is mind-blowing. I wasn't a father at the time when I wrote this, but I am now. In imagining one of my children treating me the way that the son in this story treated the father, I found that it would be exceedingly difficult for me to show the patience and the love of the father in the parable. The piece is also reflective of some of the choices that I had made when I turned away from God during my teen and young adult years, and some of the situations and experiences that I regrettably encountered because of decisions rooted in sin. I felt that using the structure most identifiable with spoken word/slam poetry would enable me to include literary devices such as internal rhymes and contemporary references to paint a more modern account of the old story that would engage a youthful audience.

Love Lifted the Prodigal

They sent out a search party but they couldn't find my body for weeks, months, and years

Fears burned the hearts of those who cared and filled theirs eyes with tears

Biological and spiritual family split right down the middle

Some chose to keep hope alive while the hope that resided in others dwindled

Eventually my protracted absence was explained away as simply just another case—

of another prodigal youth who rejected the truth he should have embraced—*should have embraced*

While they wondered, I wandered

Wild weekends with friends would tend to lead me to places where His name could not be honored

Could not be bothered with listening to the alternative choice

that was still being whispered persistently by that still small voice—*that still small voice*

A face that was moist and glistening from saltwater springing out of pain-filled eyes became an undesirable fixture in my mirror

It's strange but when friends left my side and the well with the money dried, my vision became clearer—*much clearer*

I saw myself for who I was, and I was disgusted

A selfish, gullible, thrill-seeking nobody, hustled by those he trusted

Lusted after the flesh

Dusted off for the next big spender

This foolish young offender

 was left for dead

Begging for daily bread

until the still small voice returned and said,

"Yea I have loved you with an everlasting love"—*an everlasting love*

And though in my mind I tried to fight it and override it, it was all that I could think of

It lifted me and convinced me that it was time to return

to the place where, undoubtedly, most had given up on me, but my Father was still concerned, and yearned to see me again

Out of my symbolic sinful pigpen,

I arose

in mud-covered clothes

and strode for home

A place where, when I had last left, I was dressed in the latest and best, surrounded by an entourage, but now I rolled back desperate and alone

amidst a stench that even ten bottles of David Beckham's cologne couldn't sweeten

Even in this state, love lifted me and encouraged me, and when I dragged my feet, it hurried me.

Suddenly, I realized that where I'd been and what I'd done

had never stopped Him from being my Father or me from being His son

I started to run

and love helped me to cover the last 100 meters in less than 9 seconds

without the aid of an anabolic steroid injection

I sprinted into open arms and the Ultimate Love lifted me off of my feet,

prepared a celebration feast, put me in the welcome seat

And of my past, we never speak

I approached the youth department at my church with an idea for a program that would be titled Poetry, Praise, and Hymn. The idea was to take a new approach to looking at songs found in the hymnal and present them in a poetic, instrumental, or vocal performance, or to combine elements from all three in an effort to create a fresh and original sound. For my contribution to the program, I chose to write a spoken word piece based on one of my favorite hymns, Marching to Zion. I asked a friend to sing the melody and lyrics from the chorus of recording artist Lauryn Hill's "To Zion," while I performed three stanzas of this original piece. We were accompanied by a three-piece band and a drum corps that marched in to represent the idea of the saints literally marching to Zion.

Marching to Zion

Come we that love the Lord, and let our joys be known

We have moaned and groaned and shed tears

And fought fears and lost hairs over bills

And payments in arrears and other trifling

planet earth cares for far too long

It's time to sing a new song—with sweet accord,

Dance a new step, forget and reject abject despair

March erect with pep, power, and pomp amidst our circumstance

As we advance toward the New Jerusalem

I got news for them

as in those who chose to spend their lives in

pursuit of loot,

cars, fancy dresses, and suits to look cute

truth is

the riches

in glory outweigh anything that we could purchase, mortgage, buy on credit,

lease, or rent to own

This world is not my home

I wanna live where the angels surround the throne

Those who refuse to sing couldn't know a thing about
our God
Because the children of the heavenly King seek
to speak and shout their joys abroad
Directly into your ears like a pair of Apple AirPods®
We find it odd that some who claim to be homesick
can keep their lips zipped
And look at us like misfits
while we exuberantly raise our praise to the One who
continues to sustain us on this trip—to our eternal home.
Oh, God, our help in ages past, our hope for years to come
It is the thought of seeing You face to face that helps me not to succumb
to the temptations of this place, I—become numb
and choose not to be undone
by Satan and sin. As the snare drum
provides the perfect cadence for billions of saints to march towards the
Son,
the Lamb, the Great I Am, all God, all man and
altogether holy and wonderful to me
Slowly
the things of this world become
strangely dim
I can still see them, but I no longer need them
Because my joy and my light now lie in Zion

So, let our songs abound and let every tear be dried.
No longer denied
access to Emmanuel's ground
Previously lost but now found

Let hallelujahs resound in surround sound

While—the sea of glass mass choir sings

Louder and higher than any other in history

Mysteries will unfold, the half will be told

Streets and pathways of gold

We'll love—laugh, live forever, and never grow old

No head cold or swine flu will ever confine you to your bed

"No longer will there be any curse," Revelation 22:3, I fully believe what I read.

It also said that we will serve our God and the Lamb sitting upon the throne,

I don't know about anyone else, but truth be told, I'm ready to go home.

I was asked to open a church service with a call to worship on a day run by the men's ministry department at the church that I attend. I decided to try to do something creative and unique with regard to structure while delivering content that was relevant. I wanted to speak about God's original plan for men, and how popular ideologies concerning manhood have tainted and skewed this so much that it is barely recognizable anymore. The poem is a challenge, asking, and in some ways demanding that men ignore the pressures that our flawed society places on us, and redirect our focus to the Father's perfect standard and desired role for His sons.

What Is … Men's Ministry

M-A-N

M-A-L-E

Gender signifiers that define me

Intricately created by the A1 Artist

Who sifted His holy hands through lowly sand after commanding a world into existence,

And in an instant, after an infusion of divine oxygen—free of chemical toxins—filled the lungs and exited through the nose

My perfect progenitor arose

Clothed in robes of light, the height and embodiment of God's flawless design

—but ever since—

Misguided and inquiring minds

have combined truth and error to determine why man exists

Starting with fists,

then swords, and graduating to knives, guns, and tons of other weapons of mass destruction

World leaders to street gangsters in tight white *marinas have concluded that domination through intimidation is man's primary function

Others believe that man was conceived to make money, take money, save money, and wave money in each other's faces

To flash and stash cash in offshore institutions and a variety of undetectable places

But was man really created for this?

To use our talents and gifts to attain items on selfish wish lists?

The Genesis story reveals a God in full glory making the first human being to glorify Him

Pre- and post-sin this was our earthly mission and mandate

Before and since the first date with the delectable Eve—and even after the deception—we were and are still meant to be a reflection of the Godhead in heaven,

Brethren, we were created in the image of the perfect Prototype

to be priests in our homes, and leaders in our communities, don't fall victim to the hype

that pushes us to behave according to societal stereotypes

like men shouldn't cry, show emotion, or even devotion to one woman,

Or if a man doesn't try to drive a certain car and have *'nuff children then something's wrong with him

Men, we were created and are destined for bigger and better things

For mortgage-free mansions on gold boulevards constructed by the King

So, let's sing because we're happy and worship because we're free

And exemplify the character of our Savior, which is the ultimate men's ministry

This is our call to worship.

*marinas—men's undershirts meant to be worn under other articles of clothing. Along with low-riding pants, the white marina became a staple in "street-gangster" attire.

*'nuff—Caribbean dialect, short for enough. In some instances, it can also mean "a lot."

> **But was man really created for this?**
> **To use our talents and gifts to attain items on selfish wish lists?**

Homecoming Day is a special occasion at my local church. Emphasis is placed on reaching out to individuals that have stopped attending regularly, particularly the youth, and welcoming them back to worship with us. The evening program is geared toward a younger audience, so this piece, which was performed during that time, includes slang words and phrases commonly heard in Toronto to speak directly and intimately with those in attendance. The theme of the program was Cycles which is reflected in the content of the piece. The Bible speaks about generational curses and cycles of behavior being repeated because of mistakes made by older members of a family, and the erroneous socialization of the younger ones, based on observation and poor example setting. Street life and criminal activity are used as the backdrop for this story about a family that finds itself tangled in a destructive web that leaves their present and future existence looking very bleak. Again, the literary devices found in slam poetry are employed to vividly illustrate the challenges of sin and triumph that faith in God ensures.

The Sins of the Father

Ice-cold feel of the steel from the gun against his temple

He can tell that the kid holding the *burner doesn't wanna squeeze it by the way his hands tremble

The situation is next-level stressful and any sudden moves could be detrimental

Life flashing before his eyes, his mind provides glances at circumstances from his past that were most influential

He remembers members of his family,

particularly his grandfather and his daddy

slamming dominoes, leaning back in a *bad bwoy pose

holding those *seven bones close in an effort not to expose the black dots to their foes

while sitting next to—*Ray and his nephew and a few other cold brews

with their *faces properly screwed, and he recalled thinking that when it came to being cool these dudes were pros

Then a lighter, producing a small fire would be held in front of a stick dangling from their lips and a new scent would introduce itself to his nose

They inhaled deep and exhaled a heap of smoke

Eyes red and watering, some sputtering and coughing like they were about to choke

This is what he saw some weeknights and most weekends

His family and their friends making a *fawad to their ends to participate in this habitual ritual

Smoke and drink, drink and smoke, smoke and drink—older men in his family never stopped to think about the residual

effects that their actions would have on the next generation

Ten-year-old boy taking in their every move in total and complete fascination

Spending hours and days, watching their ways and mentally repeating the phrase

"I can't wait to be just like them"

But as you know, every generation comes harder than the one before

Saw what the *older heads did and decided that he would do the same things, but add a little more

His granddaddy would smoke cigarettes and drink liquor,

His daddy would smoke cigarettes, drink liquor, and *bun weed, but he figured

that when he got bigger he would do all of the above as well, but also start to sell drugs

and earn that *Top Boy status bruv, even quicker

"Dress slicker, get richer, and *stack six figures" was his motto and his motivation

Eventually bought a mansion, three cars, and every five months or so, took a tropical vacation

His father and his grandfather were dumbfounded and perplexed by his choice of occupation

"Where did this boy get this behavior from?" oblivious to the fact that they had laid the foundation

that he built this lifestyle on,

had three sons by three women and before long—

Junior, Junior, and Junior

entered the game younger and started selling drugs sooner

than their father expected,

Used his connections and got themselves connected,

Sold more than he did, were cold-blooded, heartless, and ruthless, and on the streets they were feared and respected

Had more muscle and were way better at *the hustle than he ever was, but he refused to accept it,

Believed that the only way to correct it was to confront each Junior one by one

After all he was their father and they were his sons

And the only reason that they had what they had, and were acting so bad was because of all the things that he had done

But the first Junior that he *stepped to wasn't trying to hear his correction and pulled out a gun

Flesh and blood turned into vicious rivals

The sins of the forefathers on repeat in a four-generation deep cycle

But it's very easy for us to say that we could see this one coming from a mile away

They were a family of alcoholic abusers and drug users

No problem at all for us to look down from our righteous perch in church and brand them as sinners and eternal-life losers

However, the evil one is clever, and his deception deters a lot of us from taking responsibility and actually trying to own

The crippling cycles that we create and perpetuate based on the things we allow in our homes

How selective and subjective is our favorite's list on Netflix?

Don't use drugs, don't shoot *slugs, don't curse, but we can watch and financially endorse someone else doing it, and swear that we're not hypocrites.

Riding in our cars, we can listen to a girl or a guy glorify fornication on Spotify

But in truth if we caught two of our youth in the act somewhere in a corner in the church, we'd *cuss and cry and wonder why?

In biblical history, the children of Israel would experience victory after victory when they worshipped God, and when they rejected Him, they encountered defeat

And we do the same today, making ourselves easy prey, for the tempter's treachery and deceit

We are the working definition of insanity, doing the same things over and over and expecting different outcomes

Lying, backstabbing, giving into lust, living for us, then all shocked when we find ourselves in major problems

Cycles—stuck in a matrix, constantly taking licks, hating it, but still going back for more

Cycles—let's face it, we are sick, it's a mental health issue, it's a spiritual health issue with a cure, because my God restores

burner—gun.

bad bwoy—Jamaican/Caribbean phrase used to refer to a young man who is known for being tough or participating in criminal activity.

seven bones—seven dominoes, slang for dominoes and the number of dominoes that each player gets at the start of the game.

Ray and his nephew—Referring to Wray & Nephew, an alcoholic beverage.

faces properly screwed—to have one's "face screwed" is to have a mean look or a scowl on one's face.

fawad to their ends—Toronto urban slang meaning to go to one's home.

older heads—those from the generation before your own, or individuals that are older than you by a few years or more.

bun weed—means to smoke weed, or to smoke marijuana. "Bun" is Caribbean Creole for "burn," and "weed" is a colloquial name for the marijuana plant.

Top Boy status bruv-Reference to a show on Netflix that is popular with young people called Top Boy. The show is based in Britain and the word "bruv" is urban British slang for "bro" or "brother."

stack six figures—urban slang for having or accumulating $100,000 or more.

the hustle—slang for being involved in criminal activity in order to make a living.

stepped to—means "approached."

slugs—bullets.

cuss—in Caribbean culture the word "cuss" does not necessarily mean using curse words. "Cuss" primarily means to scold, verbally chastise, or tell someone off.

This piece was written for a special youth program called Lifeline. The program is meant to take a very direct, "no holds barred" approach to addressing Christianity and life with young people. When I was asked to write something for the program, I thought about how young people often say that they are turned off by hypocrisy in the church. I wanted to show that hypocrisy can be found in every facet of society, both inside and outside of the church, and that the only way to overcome it is to surrender your life fully to Jesus.

You Could …

You could be anything that you want to be

It's a saying, it's a motto, it's a tattoo on somebody's body, it's reality

I mean, you could smoke crack and be the mayor of a big city

You could be the ugliest person on the inside, but as long as your makeup is *on fleek, people will say that you're pretty

You could be starving yourself to be skinny and be regarded as healthy

You could have lots of money, but no family or friends and be considered wealthy

You could be an educated fool

You could hate to read or write but send and receive fifty to sixty messages a day

Barely be able to spell but, oh well, thanks to autocorrect and emojis people will still know what it is you're trying to say

"You can be anything that you want to be

It's really up to me," screams everything in society

If you are thinking critically, better yet spiritually, then you would agree that this is true

Be what you want to be, do what you want do, it's your life, it's your world, it's really all about you

Like, you can be upset, call for tougher laws and threats when a drunk driver kills a family of four

But you need drinks at parties, so you can go ahead and be happy when they make alcohol even more available by putting it in the grocery store

You could despise drug dealers and still pat *Trudeau on the back for legalizing marijuana

You could wish that you could do more to help the poor but still spend your money on massages, spa days, and saunas

You gotta have 500 dollars to spend on Big Baller basketball shoes

After all you *stay hustlin, and the struggle is real, and you should get to spend your money however you choose

Listen, this message needs to get through so I'm gonna use a cliché that a lot of pastors say which is, "you might have missed this, so let me come a little closer"

You could be prayer warrior Sabbath morning and be a *Soca warrior Saturday night

You could be a soldier in the army in the sanctuary

but if someone cuts you off for the last spot in the parking lot you can be ready to fight

You can lead out on the praise team, in beautiful musical ministry, three- or four-part harmony, perfect pitch and always on key

Then turn around and sing every sex and profanity laced song word for word alongside *Drake and Nicki.

You could wear your club and party clothes under your choir robe

You could thank God for your job, refuse to pay tithe, and use the money to vacation around the globe

You could do your best to keep all of the commandments, thou shall not steal, thou shall not commit adultery, thou shall not kill

But you could put on a movie tonight and watch other people do all those things and be very tempted to do some yourself, can you say *Netflix and chill?

You can say gambling is wrong but chip in on your office's weekly lotto

You can preach to your friends about living right, but endorse and enjoy the wrong playing *Grand Theft Auto

But this mindset is not new, the world has been telling me and you who we are, what we should be, and what we can do for far too long

Don't believe me? Check Genesis chapter 3 for the original source of this lie

When a wise guy told us straight to our face, "You can eat the fruit and you will not surely die"

So, you can gain the world, and you can lose your soul

You can compromise and try to divide your allegiance between two sides, or you can stand firm and bold

You can let the world build you up and tear down or you can plant your feet on solid ground

You can put all of your time and energy into making yourself a SnapChat or Instagram celebrity

Or you can come to Jesus to find your true identity—

Royalty, sons and daughters of the Most High on the brink of trading mortal for immortality

Thankful for Calvary, grace and mercy, what the world sees as insanity

Unapologetically Christian, unapologetically free

Unapologetically choosing to die to self so that He can live in me

Love, joy, peace, patience, kindness, goodness, gentleness, self-control— this is us—this is who we were called to be

You can get with this or you can get with that, you can choose the temporary, or you can have eternity

It's a no brainer, really.

on fleek—slang for "looking good."

tool—street slang for a gun.

*Justin Trudeau is Canada's prime minister. He made the legalization of marijuana one of his platforms when running for election. Under pressure, after he was elected, to keep his promise, he eventually legislated it on October 17, 2018.

stay hustlin—keep working hard.

Soca—musical genre created and made popular by artists in Trinidad and Tobago, now played at carnivals and in dance clubs all over the world.

Netflix and chill—a phrase used in pop culture to mean that two individuals get together to watch something on Netflix first, and then engage in sexual activity afterward.

Drake and Nicki (Manaj)—Two popular rap artists.

Grand Theft Auto—popular video game that features criminal activity.

A friend asked me to write and perform a poem at the launching of a book that he had written. The theme of the book and the event was spiritual transformation. The aim was to create a fusion between conventional rap and traditional poetry with this piece. I tried to use imagery and complex rhyme schemes to describe two different scenarios that speak to how far we stray from God and how far He is willing to extend His grace to reach us and bring us back to Him.

Grace, Grace, Grace (Grace to the 3rd Power—Father, Spirit, and Son)

"Lord, if it wasn't for Your grace where

would I be?!" He admits it, he did it, he skidded far away

from You

He started to—roll with a crew that hit the clubs

And drank the *brews on a regular

Church boy gone wild and living secular

No respecter of anything spiritual

Weekend rituals included habitual participation

in sinful sensations

Runnin' his game on girls as if their bodies were Play Stations

set up for his enjoyment

He was also involved in illegal employment

stalking the block, chillin' on corners near bus stops

selling *hot rocks to cautious customers

Neighborhood hotshot, this brother was bad,

Lord, he ignored You for years

Ignored the tears

shed by a mother whose fears

for the future of her only boy child outweighed any other

care that she could have.

He went from maintaining a straight A average to acting like a savage whose lavish lifestyle was funded by *blood money

flashed a big smile featuring a mouth full of gold teeth, but he wasn't funny
You name it, he did it, and if you had it, he took it
Forsook the straight and narrow to ride the wide and crooked.
Father, could one like this seriously expect forgiveness after
sincere repentance?
Could your grace be extended to bless a life mired in madness?

She was looking for love in all the wrong places
Searching multiple faces for traces of understanding
Started demanding
Attention by doing things that can't be mentioned
Became a new-millennium Delilah, living to hold handsome
Samsons for ransom paid after each escapade
Purchased a 2020 Cadillac Escalade with money made
working hard at what many refer to as the "oldest profession"
A lost girl with a "me against the world" expression
tattooed on her body and staining her brain
And when some tried to convince her to live otherwise, she would explain,
"I'm just doing this to pay the bills, baby"
Four kids and four fathers
frequent fornication produced one son and three daughters
that she didn't seem to care for
was never there for
Would readily ignore—if Tom, John, Sam, or any other
man came calling
Lewd, loose, and brawling, her behavior was appalling
She would do what she did daily despite her kids at home bawling
All in all, she was what most would call an undesirable
Nothing about her living could be deemed or seen as
admirable
Surely, when measured against Your law, Lord, she

would be found liable.
Death penalty by any means necessary—no chance for
survival.
But in the Bible—specifically 2 Corinthians 12 and verse 9—
the concept of "grace" is defined and outlined
It's a concept that mystifies the postmodern mind
Professors, theorists, teachers, and philosophers who find
it odd that a perfect God would offer unmerited favor to fallen humankind
Throughout the annals of history, the mystery of God's grace surfaces time after time
Murderous Moses and adulterous King David
wouldn't be saved if—
it wasn't for redeeming Grace
erasing high-stakes mistakes
The woman at the well might as well had given
up, lost in proverbial hell if grace wasn't extended
to cover her offenses
We need to come to our senses
Open our eyes wide and realize
that if wise guys
like King Solomon couldn't live their lives right and survive without
grace then what are our chances?
I'll be as candid
as I can be, speaking personally
I was buried deeper in sin than those poor *miners were in Chile
Until love lifted me and allowed me to see
Grace stretched out on a tree planted on Mount Calvary
Dying between two thieves,
Not of natural causes or a disease
But rather because of my iniquities

With every passing day, I need to fall on my knees

and proclaim

Spiritual transformation

My life's story is no better than the information that I gave you about the drug dealer or the prostitute

sinful nature condemns me to a fate dark, desperate, and destitute

Thank God for providing a way of escape from this

place

and the nightmare that would be my reality—if not for His grace.

the brews—beer.

hot rocks—illegal drugs.

blood money—money earned through illegal endeavors.

miners in Chile—referencing the incident in 2010 when thirty-three miners were trapped in a cave in Chile for over two months.

I wrote this piece to be performed for a youthful audience at another Lifeline youth program (previously mentioned). Again, popular slang phrases (some specific to youth in Toronto) were used to connect with the audience. It was written for two speakers who at times will start and finish each other's sentences, thoughts, and ideas. It is a short piece meant to be delivered with high energy and strong emphasis on repeated phrases (e.g. God first, write-off, etc.). Performed by my nephew and myself, the short message encourages us to make God the center of our lives in good and in bad times.

God First

Speaker 1: He had the *hottest whip
 and the hottest chick
 her hands around his hips
 a thousand fans on Instagram liking every single pic

Speaker 2: Loving living life above the average kid in *the 6
 Windows down, speakers blare the sounds of his favorite mix
 Summer sun, *401, collector lanes going eastbound
 Pedal to the metal, racing rebel, gonna run this town

Speaker 1: Weaving in and out of traffic, partially distracted
 By the phone, *the bars, the tracks and the volume on max
 Leaned back, relaxed now the speed reads 140
 No average Joe, he belongs in the Pro category

Speaker 2: Mind yelling *YOLO, adrenaline pumping, feeling like a promo for *Fast and
 Furious
 Pride messes with cockiness and produces the vainglorious
 Curious. GPS says fifteen more minutes, but could he make it in five?
 With his skill, this ride, and this amazing girl by his side?

Both: Right-off

Speaker 1: The once-prized ride is now a write-off

Just for a split second, girlfriend's seductive smile beckoned, he took his eyes
off
the road
Looked to the left; forgot to check the right side
Truck changing lanes then collides
with him

Speaker 2: Car starts to spin, gets hit again and again
From the rear, the left, the right, shattered headlights, the front fender falls
Right off

Speaker 1: Laying flat on his back in the hospital bed, can't take his mind off
This tragic accident, his crazy actions sent
him to the ICU and his girl to her grave
Hadn't done it in a while but in fear and despair he prayed

Speaker 2: Lord, it's been a long time since You and me had a talk
My girl is dead, can't feel my legs, but if You let me walk
I'll read my Bible and pray every day with no delay
I'll follow You, I'll follow through—on every promise, honest
You'll see, You can depend on me, my faith, our relationship will be the strongest

Speaker 1: Possibly partially paralyzed, tears in his eyes, he decides to put God first
But why do we always make this decision going forward in reverse?
Lose your job, call on God

Speaker 2: Bill is due today, start to pray

Speaker 1: Got a disease, get on your knees

Speaker 2: But when life is sweet, get back on your feet

Speaker 1: God first after disaster

Speaker 2: God first in sorrow not laughter
God first when dreams are shattered

Speaker 1: God first when you lose everything that mattered

Speaker 2: God first—something to say in between failure and being redeemed
Spoken time and again, but are we really taking in what it means?

Speaker 1: God first means unpopular decisions
God first means living like a full-time Christian
God first means your religion may need redefinition
God first means your life may end up differently than you envisioned

Speaker 2: Not an easy task but when you put God first
A life that's blessed and a robe of righteousness is what it's worth.

*hottest whip—nicest car.

*the 6—name for Toronto made popular by rapper Drake which refers to the last digit of the city's area code, 416.

*401—longest, busiest highway in Toronto.

*the bars, the tracks—music, particularly rap music.

*YOLO—acronym in youth culture that reached its peak in popularity between 2012-2016 meaning You Only Live Once.

*Fast and Furious—popular film series consisting of nine parts.

TEACH Services, Inc.
P U B L I S H I N G

We invite you to view the complete
selection of titles we publish at:
www.TEACHServices.com

We encourage you to write us
with your thoughts about this,
or any other book we publish at:
info@TEACHServices.com

TEACH Services' titles may be purchased in
bulk quantities for educational, fund-raising,
business, or promotional use.
bulksales@TEACHServices.com

Finally, if you are interested in seeing
your own book in print, please contact us at:
publishing@TEACHServices.com

We are happy to review your manuscript at no charge.

www.ingramcontent.com/pod-product-compliance
Lightning Source LLC
Chambersburg PA
CBHW070544170426
43200CB00011B/2555